MW00579405

Internationally acclaimed bestselling author RJ Parker is most well known for his books, TOP CASES of The FBI (Winner of the World Book Awards 2012), Unsolved Serial Killings and Women Who Kill. He has seven true crime books available in eBook, paperback and audiobook formats.

Canadian Author RJ Parker was born and raised in Newfoundland and now resides in Oshawa and Newfoundland, Canada. RJ started writing after becoming disabled with Anklyosing Spondylitis eight years ago, but only recently published. He spent 30 years in various facets of Government and has two professional designations. RJ is a proud dad of two girls, as well as twin sons. RJ also consults with Police Departments when requested.

To date, RJ has donated over 1,500 books to allied troops serving overseas and to our wounded warriors recovering in Naval and Army hospitals all over the world.

CONTACT INFORMATION:

WWW. RJPARKER.NET
AUTHORRJPARKER@GMAIL.COM

Other True Crime e-books by this Author
Available in eBooks, Audiobooks and
Paperbacks

Unsolved Serial Killings
Women Who Kill
Top Cases of The FBI
Cold Blooded Killers
Doctors Who Killed
Case Closed: Serial Killers Captured
Rampage Spree Killers

ACKNOWLEDGEMENTS

I thank my daughters Amanda and Katie who encourages me everyday. Without them, I may have given up to my disability and the chronic pain that goes with it. For those who have AS or any arthritic problem especially in their spine and hips, they know what I'm talking about.

To my many fans and friends on FaceBook, thank you.

My grandson Parker Joseph was born on October 17, 2012 and he is my pride and joy.

My business partners Bernard Lee DeLeo and Dane Ladwig, you guys really are the best. I love you both like brothers.

Chapter 1
Serial Killer Defined

A serial killer, as characteristically defined, is a person who has murdered three or more people over a period with a cooling off period between the murders. The motive for killing is typically based on psychological gratification. Many serial killers who are caught usually do not see a prison cell, but are put in a mental facility instead. Some sources label serial killing as a series of two or more murders, committed in separate events, by one criminal acting alone, or simply a minimum of at least two murders.

The FBI states that motives for serial murder include thrill, anger, rage, financial profit, and attention seeking, but often there is a sexual factor involved. In addition, a serial killer will normally target people who have something in common such as appearance (blonde-haired people with blue eyes), occupation (prostitutes), race (colored people), sex (females), or age groups (teenagers).

Serial Killers are not spree killers, someone who kills two or more people without a cooling off period, nor are they mass murderers, a person or a group who kills more than four people at one event.

The FBI defines serial murder as follows:

* A minimum of three victims, with periods of "cooling off" in between.
* The killer is usually a stranger to the victim, and the murders appear random.
* The murders reflect a need to viciously dominate the victim.
* The murder is rarely "for profit;" the motive is psychological, not material.
* The victims may have "metaphorical" significance for the killer.
* Killers often choose victims who are vulnerable: prostitutes, runaways, etc.
* The typical serial killer is a white male from a lower to middle class background, habitually in his twenties or thirties. Several were bodily or psychologically abused by

parents. As children, serial killers often set fires, torture animals, and wet their beds; these red flag behaviors are known as the triad of signs. Brain injuries are often common. Many are above intelligent and have revealed immense promise as successful people. They are also captivated with police and authority in general. They either will have endeavored to become police officers themselves but were rejected, or be employed as security guards, or have served in the military. Many of them, including John Wayne Gacy, Ted Bundy, and the Hillside Strangler, would camouflage themselves as law enforcement officials in order to gain entrance to their victims.

Attributes

* Over 90 percent of serial killers are white males.
* They have a propensity to be intelligent, with above-average IQs.
* Despite their high IQs, most do poorly in school and have difficulty in holding a job.

* Classically, they are neglected as children and were raised by domineering mothers.
* There is often a family history of psychiatric and alcoholic issues.
* They are generally abused mentally and sexually as children.
* A lot of them end up spending time in reform schools as children.
* They have a higher than normal rate of suicide attempts.
* From an early age, they have interests in fetishism, voyeurism, and pornography.
* Over 60% of serial killers were wetting their beds past the age of twelve.
* Fire starting: their attraction with fire is an early demonstration of their fondness for dramatic destruction. Otis Toole, the associate of Henry Lee Lucas, burned down a neighborhood house when he was just six years old. Teenage adventure killer George Adorno was only four years old when he first displayed his pyromaniac tendencies, setting fire to his own sister. The habitual Carl Panzram was thrown into a reformatory when he was only eleven years old, and just months after torched the place, causing

damage in excess of over one hundred thousand dollars.

* Sadistic activity: serial killers get their enjoyment from tormenting small animals at an early age, later graduating from animals to human beings.

Chapter 2
Organized or Disorganized

One of the many jobs of an FBI profiler is classifying the UNSUB or Unknown Subject, collecting facts about the crimes he or she committed for understanding and future knowledge. FBI profiler, John Douglas, termed the words 'disorganized' and 'organized' in the study of serial killers. These differences can be contingent from facts and other information about the crime, or from the crime scene itself.

A disorganized, psychotic, or mentally ill individual, is inferred from a messy, disorganized crime scene with lots of evidence left behind. On the other hand, an organized killer, someone who shows no remorse, and is psychopathic, is controlled, planning, premeditated, and leaves behind very little, if any, evidence at a crime scene.

Organized Serial Killer Attributes:

IQ above average; 105-120 range
Socially adequate
Lives with partner or dates frequently
Stable father figure
Harsh family physical abuse
Geographically/occupationally mobile
Follows the news media
May be college educated
Good hygiene/housekeeping skills
Does not usually keep a hiding place
Diurnal (daytime) habits
Drives a flashy car
Needs to return to crime scene to see what police have done
Usually contacts police to play games
A police groupie
Doesn't experiment with self-help
Kills at one site, disposes at another
May dismember body
Attacks using seduction, into restraints
Doesn't dehumanize victims
Leaves a controlled crime scene
Leaves little physical evidence
Responds best to direct interview

Disorganized Serial Killer Attributes:

IQ below average, 80-95 range
Socially inadequate
Lives alone, usually does not date
Absent or unstable father
Family emotional abuse, inconsistent
Lives and/or works near crime scene
Minimal interest in news media
Usually a high school dropout
Poor hygiene/housekeeping skills
Keeps a secret hiding place in the home
Nocturnal (nighttime) habits
Drives a clunky car or pickup truck
Needs to return to crime scene for reliving memories
May contact victim's family to play games
No interest in police work
Experiments with self-help programs
Kills at one site, considers mission over
Usually leaves body intact
Attacks in a "blitz" pattern
Depersonalizes victim to a thing or it
Leaves a chaotic crime scene
Leaves physical evidence
Responds best to counseling interview

Noteworthy Facts

* H.H. Holmes, America's First Serial Killer, was convicted of nine murders; however, Holmes confessed to twenty-seven murders, and some investigators thought he might have actually murdered hundreds. When the World's Fair opened in Chicago in 1893, he began by killing guests at the enormous Castle Hotel. His crimes were discovered in an inspection after a janitor told police that he was not permitted to clean certain floors of the hotel. He was convicted and hanged three years later in 1896.

* Most of the victims of Jeffrey Dahmer and John Wayne Gacy, who were both white males, were men and boys of racial or ethnic minorities.

* Mary Bell was only ten years old when she was convicted of murdering two boys in England in 1968. After being confined first in an all-boys' reform school, she was later sent to a women's prison and was released

at the age of twenty-three.

* The Son of Sam, David Berkowitz, was a thrill killer who enjoyed the excitement of the kill. He did not touch any of his fifteen victims, but instead followed and shot at them from a distance.

* Most serial killers are white males between the ages of twenty and thirty-five. In recent years, however, there has been an increase of serial killers from other races.

* The USA makes up 76% of the world's serial killers. England has produced 28% of the European total.

* The western part of the United States such as California and Washington has produced more serial killers than any other part of the United States.

* Serial killers are often quite intelligent with an above average IQ.

* At any given time in the U.S., there are

thirty to fifty unidentified active serial killers at work constantly changing their targets and methods; however, some authorities think that number is much higher.

* Runaways, prostitutes, and others who lead covert lives are usually not reported missing immediately and receive little police or media attention. This makes them extraordinary targets for killers.

* Experts hypothesize on what happens to unsolved cases of murderers. It is believed that some commit suicide, die, are imprisoned for other crimes, are put in mental institutions, move to another locations, or simply stop killing. Rarely do they turn themselves in.

* The term serial killer was coined in the 1970s by the FBI.

* Serial killers often suffer from Antisocial Personality Disorder, APD, and appear to be ordinary or even polite. Sometimes this is referred to as the mask of sanity. There's

often sexual characteristic to the murders, and killers may have a fondness for a particular gender, occupation, appearance, race, or other choices.

* As children, serial killers usually experience a significant amount of psychological, physical, and sexual abuse. Many times, it is a combination of all three. This vicious exploitation helps to motivate in them intense feelings of embarrassment and helplessness, which they usually impose upon their later victims.

* Many serial killers have a voracious appetite for unusual sexuality, and obsessions with fetishism, voyeurism, and aggressive pornography.

* Serial killers often have a comfort zone, committing their crimes to some extent close to their homes and prefer to hunt for their victims at places they are familiar with, where they feel in control. They know the best spots in the area to capture victims, and the quickest getaway routes.

Chapter 3
Capturing Serial Killers

How are serial killers caught? A killer continues to kill until he or she either is captured, dies, is put in jail for another crime, stops killing, or kills him or herself. After any homicide is committed, there is a thorough crime scene investigation and routine autopsies done on the victim, as well as many other steps in solving the crime.

Once all of this information has been collected, it is entered into a nationwide database run by the FBI as part of ViCAP (Violent Criminal Apprehension Program). This program can help determine different patterns, or signatures, that can link separate homicides done anywhere in the country.

A signature is a ritual, something the subject does intentionally for emotional satisfaction, something that is not necessary to perpetuate the crime. Some serial killers pose their victims in a certain way, or leave them in a certain place or position after killing them. This is an example of a signature. Another example might be a method of torture or dismembering. In short, it is what the killer does to accomplish his fantasies, and it can tell investigators a great deal about his personality and if he or she is organized or disorganized killer, which would also reflect on the intelligence of the killer.

Another method used in catching a serial killer is the establishment of an MO, or Modus Operandi, for the crime. The MO reflects the killer's habits and what the killer had to do to commit the crime. This includes everything from luring and restraining his victim to the way that he actually murders; for example: their habitual choice of weapon. A serial killer's MO can change over time. Essentially, he or she learns from past blunders and improves with time. These are some of the components of criminal profiling.

Profiling Serial Killers

The Federal Bureau of Investigation developed the Behavioral Sciences Unit in 1972, using both signatures and MOs as aspects of profiling. Studies by psychologists and psychiatrists, and information gleaned from past serial murders, are compiled in the creation of a profile, along with crime scene information and witness statements. For example, if the victim is Caucasian, the killer is most likely Caucasian also, and if the crime scene demonstrates evidence of careful planning, the killer is most likely to be older, intelligent, and organized. A lot of it is theoretical, based on several studies and interviews of serial killers. Profiles are rarely 100% precise, but they are usually found to be very close.

After all the variables are compiled to make a profile, investigators can look at the existing list of suspects and ascertain which are most likely to have committed the crime and determine how best to apprehend him/her. Some organized serial killers, such as Dennis Rader, The BTK Killer, feel the need to mock the police, which sometimes leads to their arrest. In Rader's case, he sent police a floppy disk containing data that was traced to his church. Many serial killers are unbelievably controlled and methodical, but also so arrogant that they slip up in some way that leads to their arrest. Jeffrey Dahmer, for instance, let a victim escape who then led police directly to Dahmer's apartment.

Not all serial killers are caught however, and in this book there are several unsolved serial killing cases. Yes, some are arrested or picked up for other crimes, and evidence leads investigators to their murders, but other times it's just pure luck for the authorities or bad luck for the serial killer, that leads to their capture. For example, Ted Bundy was caught at a routine traffic stop, while David Berkowitz, The Son of Sam, was initially picked up for loitering and was thought to be a witness to the crimes instead of the killer.

Most serial killers either spend their lives in prison once convicted, or are executed if the death penalty exists in the state that prosecuted them. Of course, there's always the exception to the rule. For instance, Ed Gein was considered incompetent to stand trial and was sent to a mental facility, but his doctor later determined him to fit. The judge then found him not guilty because of insanity, and in 1984, he died of heart failure in prison.

Peter Woodcock is an example of no cure for a serial killer. He spent thirty-five years in a criminal ward at a psychiatric hospital in Ontario, Canada, after killing three children. Only hours after being released, he killed another psychiatric patient and was immediately sent back to the hospital. He'd been released as he was deemed cured by his psychiatrist, but obviously, even after thirty-five years, he was not cured.

Chapter 4
Female Serial Killers

Female serial killers often remain unobserved, hiding in the background, masked by her male equal. Her acts are unusual and uncommon, but never fail. She behaves in a more delicate and precise manner, and is deadly and merciless. The most common of her monstrous crimes have not yet been comprehended. The theory of the female serial killer herself still lies within the specialty of uncertainty. It is time, however, to capture this hushed serial killer and bring her crimes to our attention.

What is the difference between a serial murderer from any other murderer? A murderer is usually defined as someone who takes the life of another person. A serial murderer usually murders more than three people.

Although the time phase within which the killer is performing may be the subject of debate, criminologists and researchers usually agree on a definition of serial murderer as a person who engages in the murdering of three or more people in a period of thirty days or more.

Although this definition is adequate in the identification of a serial murderer, it does not differentiate between male and female perpetrators. There are however, differences between the sexes. The average period of vigorous killing for females is eight years. For males, it is only about four years.

Female serial killers seldom torture their victims or commit any violence on their victims' bodies. Female killers prefer weapons that are difficult to distinguish, such as poison, fatal injections, and induced accidents.

The sort of victims chosen by female serial killers further reveal a dissimilar typology from male serial murders. Male killers, usually acting as sexual predators, tend to mark adult female victims. Female killers, however, seldom choose their prey based on sex, and usually attack victims that are familiar to her, such as children, relatives, and spouses. Sometimes, if she does turn against a stranger, it is usually one who can be conquered easily, such as an older person under her care or even a child.

The average age of the female serial killer's first victim is fourteen to sixty-four. The typical female serial murderer commences killing after the age of twenty-five. The female serial killer is more multifaceted than the male and is often harder to catch. Since the definition of the serial killer is insufficient in explaining this quiet female killer, classifying her becomes a requirement in fully comprehending both her and the temperament of her crimes.

According to FBI Profiler, Robert K. Ressler, both male and female serial killers may be classified in one of two groupings: the 'organized' and the 'disorganized.' The organized killer usually exhibits qualities of high intelligence and sociability, a stable employment history, normal sexual functioning, and an outstanding ability of controlling her emotions during the act of murder. On the contrary, the disorganized killer has average intelligence, underdeveloped social skills, a turbulent employment history, and sexual dysfunction.

Although this evaluation might be helpful, it still sheds very little light towards understanding female serial killers. As female and male serial killers have very little in common, making classifications that apply to both sexes rather futile. Female serial killers usually come under any one of the following categories: Black Widow, Angel of Death, Sexual Predator, Revenge, Profit, Team Killer, Question of Sanity, or Unexplained and Unsolved.

Chapter 5
The Black Widows

The Black Widow is one of the most lethal female serial killers, very organized and successful in her killings. A Black Widow is defined as a woman who systematically murders a number of spouses, family members, children, or individuals outside the family with whom she has established a close relationship. She commonly begins her deadly career in her late twenties and may be active for a whole decade before giving rise to any suspicions.

Her crimes are revealed only after the increasing number of deaths around her may no longer be discarded as coincidences. The victims of the Black Widow usually number between six and ten; their ages and sex are generally unimportant. Her methodology ranges between poison, suffocation, strangulation, and shooting, though poison is the most favored of her methods, used 87% of the time.

The Black Widow kills for two motives. The first: profit. In fact, the overwhelming majority of Black Widows are lured into murder by the proceeds of life insurance or the assets of the victim. Usually, a monetary windfall will eventually fall into the possession of the perpetrator after the victim's death. In fact, it is not uncommon for these women to insure the victims themselves shortly before they execute a crime, thus giving substantial proof of how calculating, methodical, and devious, a female serial killer can be.

Belle Gunness is probably one of the earliest and most notorious Black Widows. Gunness was born in 1859 in Norway as Brynhild Paulsdatter Storset. At the age of twenty-one, already showing signs of her ambitions, she immigrated to the United States and changed her name to Bella.

In 1884, she met Mads Sorenson who was also a Norwegian immigrant. Marrying a year later, Gunness settled into what could be considered an uneventful decade until her love for money – and the lack of it – drove her to extremes in 1896. In that year, she and her husband opened a confectionery shop which was mysteriously destroyed by a fire caused by a kerosene lamp – a lamp that was inexplicably never found. Around that same time, their oldest child, Caroline, suddenly died of what medical personnel believed to be acute colitis.

Insurance profits from both incidents proved sufficient to alleviate the pain of the grieving mother, who used the money to buy a new house. Surprisingly enough, the new house also burned down in 1898, a misfortune that was soon followed by the death of another child, Alex. Gunness received yet another insurance settlement and this time, too, she used the money to buy a new house. In 1900, Mads Sorenson suddenly died of an undiagnosed ailment that exhibited the symptoms of strychnine poisoning.

This unexplained death also passed unobserved, and Gunness used the money from the insurance to buy a farm for her and her three surviving children. Two years later, in 1902, Gunness married another

Norwegian immigrant named Peter Gunness. The marriage was short lived; in 1903 Gunness would be a widow again. Peter died when a sausage grinder happened to fall from a shelf and strike him on the head as he was passing underneath.

Shortly after this tragic event, Gunness began to hire local laborers to help her with the farm. Unfortunately, most of them disappeared mysteriously. In 1906, Gunness' stepdaughter, Jennie Olsen, also disappeared. She was allegedly sent to a school in California. In 1908, the Gunness' farmhouse was destroyed by a fire of, again, unexplained origin. Investigators searching the house for signs of arson found the bodies of three children and an adult female in the basement. Oddly enough, the woman's body was decapitated and investigators could not locate the head.

The remains of other mutilated bodies were found throughout the farm. Ray Lamphere, who had worked on the Gunness' farm, was arrested and charged with arson and murder. Even though the exact number of victims was never identified, it is believed to have numbered anywhere between sixteen and twenty-eight. Lamphere argued that Gunness was the one who had set the fire and that she was the person responsible for forty-nine murders.

According to his testimony, Gunness was alive; he had helped her escape. He further argued that the decapitated body belonged to an unfortunate woman who had been lured to the farm with money. To this day, we do not know whether Gunness died in the fire or whether she had managed to commit the perfect crime and elude being apprehended.

Even though the Black Widow, murdering for profit, might appear to be unparalleled by any other serial killer, the type of Black Widow that murders out of jealousy and rejection is equally merciless. This type of Black Widow is epitomized in the person of Vera Renczi.

Vera Renczi was born in 1903 in Hungary. She suffered from a pathological fear of rejection that eventually led to a series of murders that lasted throughout her adult life. She murdered thirty-five individuals, including her husbands, lovers, and son. By the age of sixteen, she had run away with several local men considerably her senior.

Like all her relationships, Renczi's marriage to a local executive did not last more than a brief period. Her pathological jealousy found expression in frequent and violent fits of anger against her mate, and soon her husband disappeared mysteriously. Renczi remarried shortly afterwards, but her new husband disappeared as well after Renczi convinced herself of his infidelity.

Throughout the following years, Renczi acquired a number of lovers – thirty-two to be exact – all of whom mysteriously disappeared from her life. The vicious Black Widow became so obsessed that she did not hesitate to take the life of her own son once he had discovered the truth about her vanishing lovers and husbands.

The fact that her own son had dared to blackmail her marked the ultimate form of treachery in Renczi's eyes. After murdering thirty-five victims, Renczi was finally discovered when the wife of one of her lovers became suspicious and called the police when her husband failed to return home. Renczi admitted to lifelong deadly practices and led the police to the basement of her home where the remains of thirty-five men were preserved in lavish zinc coffins. Each one of the victims was poisoned by lethal doses of arsenic.

Chapter 6
The Angels of Death

The Angels of Death are the lethal caretakers who match, by all standards, the Black Widows in their viciousness. These are the women from whom the elderly seek support, and to whom parents trust their children. Because these women usually act in places where death is a common occurrence, such as hospitals, they not only pass unobserved, but it is often very hard to determine the exact number of victims.

One thing, however, is certain, the Angel of Death targets victims who are unable to shield or defend themselves, and who are, in her own eyes, already condemned to die. The Angel of Death, like the Black Widow, uses a weapon that is delicate and hard to detect. When the victim is an adult, she uses deadly injections of chemicals such as potassium, which will cause a heart attack. When the victims are young children, she resorts to suffocation, usually with a pillow.

She usually starts killing in her twenties, making bold decisions over who is to live and who is to die, and just might maintain this habit over a long period in her life. A classic Angel of Death exhibits two characteristics that usually make her apprehension a little easier. The first is that she is obsessive in her need to kill, and she kills repetitively within her own area of responsibility – such as a nurse or caretaker.

The second is that the Angel of Death often enjoys talking about her crimes in an attempt to gloss them over as acts of mercy, and often tries to depict herself as a heroine and caring benefactor. Angels of Death are usually highly regarded by their co-workers, supervisors, and even their own victims' relatives.

Even though numerous Angels of Death are responsible for taking the lives of hundreds of innocent children and helpless elderly people throughout the last quarter of the century, very few of them have actually been apprehended.

One of the most villainous Angels of

Death was Genene Jones, an American nurse born in 1951. She was actively criminal between the ages of twenty-seven to thirty-one, and was responsible for the death of at least eleven children, all of them injected with lethal chemicals. It was suspected that she might have been involved in the deaths of as many as forty-six children.

Having changed jobs from the Bexar County Medical Center in San Antonio, Texas, to the Kerr County clinic, and then to the Sip Peterson Hospital, she allowed suspicions to rise as the numbers of infant deaths in each hospital frighteningly increased while she worked there. Unfortunately, changing location also provided her with ample time to carry out the killings that satisfied her perverted need for power, control, and recognition. She was finally caught and brought before justice in 1984. She received a sentence of ninety-nine years in prison. The exact number of her victims is still unknown to this day.

Chapter 7
Sexual Predators and Revenge

The sexual predator is the rarest crime committed by a woman. It is so rare that American criminal history has only one reported female sexual predator who was acting alone, and that is Aileen Wuornos. She was an American serial killer who, between 1989 and 1990, killed seven men in Florida. She claimed they raped her while she was working as a prostitute. Wuornos was convicted and sentenced to death for six of the murders and executed by lethal injection on October 9, 2002.

The term sexual predator is used critically to describe a person seen as obtaining or trying to obtain sexual contact with another person in a figuratively predatory manner. A female sexual predator is thought to hunt for her sex prey. Rapists and child sexual abusers are usually referred to as sexual predators, particularly in the media.

In contrast to the Black Widows, the Angels of Death, and the Sexual Predators, the fourth category of female serial killers is the Revenge Serial Killer. Whereas it is not hard to understand why a resentful, vengeful female, might take on a single act of murder, it is exceptionally complex to understand why she would engage in a series of murders.

Traditionally, crimes that are motivated by extreme hatred are crimes that are targeted against a particular individual or individuals, and are thus rarely serial in nature. They also take place within a limited framework of time, when the feelings involved are strong enough to motivate a murder.

There are also crimes of passion which are both deliberate and carefully calculated in their execution. In the case of serial murders, however, feelings of anger remain highly personalized even when the victims vary. That is especially so because the perpetrator holds her victims responsible for whatever may cause her hostility, and she attacks them as a symbolic act of retribution. As a result, there is an overpowering steadiness among the revenge serial killer's victims, which are often tragically her own children, murdered in a perverted attempt to hurt her spouse.

Like the Black Widow, she prefers suffocation or poison, but her crimes are not carried out with the persistency and precision of the Black Widow. That can be attributed to the fact that the revenge serial killer is a victim of her own feelings, acting impulsively, which could explain why she shows immense remorse after she is caught.

Chapter 8
Murder for Profit

Women who Murder for Profit must clearly kill for profit and must target victims outside their family. She is also very well organized, hard to discern, and may be active for a number of years before she is actually apprehended. The average number of her victims can be as high as thirty people, and she is usually active for ten to fifteen years unless captured before then. Usually, she begins her lethal career in her mid-twenties, and, like the Black Widow, she prefers poison.

Like the Angels of Death, she also has a highly dispassionate approach to murder. Like the sexual predator, she is fearful and vicious, and like the revenge serial killer, she is highly motivated. Nevertheless, she is distinctive in that she kills for somebody else, usually abused wives that pay her to free them from their torturing husbands.

The first known case of a female

serial killer who had turned murder into a profitable business was that of a Russian, the notorious Madame Popova. Little is known about her crimes, except that she operated in Czarist Russia between 1880 and 1909. According to her own confession, Popova was responsible for the murder of three-hundred men whose spouses had paid a humble fee in order to free themselves from their brutality. Popova sent those men to death by using poison. Her business was a successful one for nearly thirty years, until one of her clients, in an attack of remorse, confessed to the police. Popova was arrested and subsequently confessed to her crimes.

Chapter 9
Female Team Killers

All the female serial killers that have been discussed so far are distinguished by the fact that they operate under their own initiatives and primarily carry out their deadly activities on their own. It is estimated, however, that only one third of female serial killers act alone.

The remaining two-thirds commit homicides within the context of a team. There are different types of serial killing teams: the female-male, the female-female, and the family. The male-female teams are the most common, and are usually active for a substantial period since the two members are commonly lovers and therefore tend to agree and co-operate more. Furthermore, the female subjects herself to the direction of the male who then becomes the prevailing partner. The homicides committed by the couple are often well organized, and the female involved is considerably younger than any of her female serial killer counterparts, typically around the age of twenty at the time of her first murder.

Bonnie and Clyde, the most notorious criminal couple, were a serial killing team. Even though they were not as lethal as some modern couples, Bonnie and Clyde will always be the depression era duo that shook the world.

Traditionally, female-female serial killer teams are the second most prolific of the team killers. Although their motives may vary, the killings are usually carried out for profit and use weapons such as, poison, lethal injections, and suffocation.

Gwendolyn Graham and Catherine May Wood's crimes in the Alpine Manor Nursing Home in the 1980s are an example of the female-female killing band. In 1986, Catherine May Wood became supervisor of nurse's aides at the Alpine Manor nursing home in Walker, Michigan. At the time she was only twenty-four and weighed 450 pounds. After her seven-year marriage had dissolved, she met Graham who had just received a job in the nursing home as Wood's supervisor, and fell deeply in love with her new.

Wood, who once again felt both wanted and needed, immediately surrendered herself to Graham's dominance and perverted sexual desires. Unfortunately, her desires included committing murders with the aim of enhancing their sexual encounters. Their sexual relationship had already involved rough play and choking for some time, and Graham apparently wanted to experience the real thing. Even though Wood discarded her mate's abnormal ideas as mere talk, the ideas soon materialized as reality. In January of 1987, Graham attacked and murdered her first victim, the beginning of a macabre plan that aimed at taking the lives of six elderly people whose last names spelled 'murder.'

The plan however, proved too elaborate and soon the two lovers settled into targeting the most vulnerable victims. Within four months, the women attacked ten patients of the nursing home and succeeded in killing five of them. Graham used a dampened washcloth to kill her patients while Wood acted as a lookout. After each murder, the women would make love in a vacant area of the nursing home, aiming to relive the excitement of the act of murder.

By April of 1987, the couple's murderous acts ended when Graham and Wood argued over Wood's failure to actively engage her in any of the murders. By this time, Graham had already found another lover and soon left Wood. Alone and deserted again, Wood confessed the murders to her ex-husband, who contacted the authorities. Wood and Graham were then arrested and Wood pleaded guilty, agreed to testify against Graham, and received a sentence of twenty to forty years in prison. Graham received six life sentences without the possibility of parole.

Three or more individuals who may or may not be biologically related comprise family serial killing teams. Regardless of their biological relationship, they typically live in the same house and act like a family. The dominant figure is usually a male and the team commonly engages itself in sexual serial murders that tend to be extremely violent. The active period of the team tends to be rather short, since relationships between members and co-operation collapse very easily, leading to disorganization and final apprehension.

Charles Manson, born in 1934 in Kentucky, can be argued to be one of the most perverted minds the American Criminal history has ever seen. Being both articulate and extremely intelligent, Manson was able to gather around him a group of rebellious young females and males to form the family that he never really had, a family that soon turned into a growing cult. The Manson family engaged in marathon sessions of unrestricted sex and drug use. At its peak, the family numbered fifty members, all of whom earned their living from a variety of illegal activities. The family eventually settled into an abandoned film studio ranch in California, where Manson continued to poison the minds of his young followers with an incessantly more aggressive philosophy that escalated to the beginning of a brutal murder spree.

All of the victims were stabbed and shot, and Sharon Tate, who was eight month pregnant at the time, was stabbed and hanged by the neck. In both cases, the blood of the victims were used to mark the crime scene. Two months later the police arrested a number of the Manson family members for an unrelated minor offense. Among those arrested was Susan Atkins, twenty-one, who was present in both the Tate and the LaBianca murders.

While Atkins was in custody, she began discussing details of the murders with her cellmates, conversations that helped seal the deal of the family's criminal activities. Several members of the family were found guilty of murder and sentenced to death. The sentences, however, were commuted to life imprisonment when the Supreme Court overturned the death penalty. After the trial, members of the family who had not been arrested continued the murders of many individuals, including Manson's defense attorney. More than twenty murders are now associated to the Manson Family and the cult that Manson had created around his name.

Chapter 10
Issue of Sanity

The insane serial killer is a very subtle and controversial case as the perpetrator cannot be held responsible for his actions. This is why it is necessary to establish what differentiates an insane person from a sane person. To claim insanity is rarely valid in cases of serial murder since a sequence of murders requires both planning and a clear state of mind in order to avoid apprehension. Given the heinous nature of her crimes, the female serial killer is usually considered legally sane.

In the rare case where a female perpetrator is acknowledged to have been insane, the serial killer was always an Angel of Death suffering from Munchausen syndrome by proxy, a mental disorder where caregivers deliberately exaggerate, fabricate, and/or bring on physical, psychological, behavioral, and mental health problems in others.

Bobbie Sue Terrell, at the age of twenty-two, began her nursing career in 1976. Shortly afterwards she married Daniel Dudley, but her happiness was shattered when she learned she could not have any children. She reacted to the news with a combination of anger and depression, which did not seem to go away even after they adopted a boy. As her depression and violent anger increased, she was forced to seek professional help and was put under the treatment of strong tranquilizers. The medication further deteriorated Terrell's situation. She fed a nearly lethal dose of the tranquilizers to her own son. Fortunately, the boy survived, but this incident marked the end of her marriage.

Abandoned, confused, and suffering from manic depression, Terrell admitted herself to a mental hospital for the treatment of schizophrenia. After a year, she was released and was able to return to her profession as a nurse. She remained unable, however, to control her emotions that worsened in the stressful environment of the hospital. Her unusual behavior culminated in 1984 with the sudden death of ninety-nine-year-old Aggie Marsh, Terrell's first known victim. Within thirteen days, Terrell succeeded in killing twelve elderly people by injecting them with lethal doses of insulin. On November twenty-fourth, 1984, local police received an anonymous call claiming that a serial killer was operating in the hospital staff.

Upon arrival, they found Terrell suffering from a severe knife wound on her side that had been allegedly inflicted by the serial killer. Investigators, however, could find no other staff that could support Terrell's story. Although Terrell's mental history and her suffering from the Munchausen Syndrome by proxy was brought to light, it was not until 1985 that all the pieces were put together. She was finally arrested in 1985 and charged with murder. For the next three years, she was subjected to a number of psychological tests, all of which pointed towards her insanity. She was finally charged with a single count of murder, found guilty, and sentenced to sixty-five years in prison.

Chapter 11
The Unexplained Killer

The motive of the 'unexplained' serial killer has never been satisfactorily understood even after the perpetrator was discovered and arrested. A female perpetrator can fit the category of the unexplained if she is "a woman who systematically murders for reasons that are wholly inexplicable or for a motive that has not been made sufficiently clear for categorization." In the great majority of these situations, even the killer herself is unable to identify an understandable motive for her crimes.

Christine Falling, as is often the case with serial killers, had a disruptive and impoverished childhood. She was born in Florida in 1963, to sixteen year-old Ann and sixty-five year old Thomas Slaughter. Falling was developmentally disabled, prone to obesity, suffered from fits of epilepsy and aggression, and was never able to acquire developmental skills beyond those of a sixth grader. Due to the extreme poverty of her parents, Falling and her older sister were given up for adoption to the Falling family. Not long afterwards, the two girls found themselves in a children's home due to their constant conflicts with their adoptive parents. By that time, Falling had already demonstrated her violent nature, her favorite pastime being the torturing and killing of cats to see if they really had nine lives. At the age of twelve, Falling left the children's home. Two years later she married a man ten years older than her, but the marriage soon collapsed after a series of violent encounters between the couple.

That sparked off new and mysterious behavior in Falling. Within the next couple of years she visited the hospital multiple times with an endless series of medical conditions that medical staff was never able to diagnose. Despite the fact that Falling was apparently suffering from mental illnesses, she had gained a status as a good baby-sitter.

At the age of seventeen, however,

Falling began to attack and murder the children that were placed under her care. On February twenty-eighth, 1980, Cassidy Johnson, two years old, died from what was assumed encephalitis. Autopsy reports showed that the girl had actually succumbed to a brutal skull injury. The police interviewed Falling, but since no evidence could be brought against her, the matter was not pursued. Shortly afterwards, Falling moved to Lakeland, Florida, where she killed another baby under her care.

Even though the death of four-year-old Jeffrey Davis was also deemed suspicious, no widespread investigation was carried out, allowing Falling to attack a new victim. Within three days after Jeffrey's death, Falling was asked to baby-sit Jeffrey's two year-old cousin, Joseph Spring, while the bereaved family attended Jeffrey's funeral. Joseph's death was attributed to a viral infection, and thus Falling once again escaped capture. After the double murder, Falling moved to Perry, Florida where she found a job as a housekeeper in the home of seventy-seven year-old, William Swindle.

On the first day of her job, Swindle suddenly died in his kitchen. Due to his old age and his deteriorating health, there was no suspicion of foul play, and Falling continued her killings. Her next victim was her eighteen-month-old niece who allegedly stopped breathing while under Falling's care. Once again, the vicious serial killer was able to escape apprehension. A year later, in 1982, Travis Coleman, only ten weeks old, also stopped breathing while Falling was attending to him. An autopsy was requested, and it was discovered that the infant had died from suffocation. The authorities immediately questioned Falling and she confessed to having killed Travis and three other babies as well by what she described as 'smotheration.' According to her testimony, she'd heard voices that had ordered her to kill the babies by placing a blanket over their faces.

Falling was found guilty of these murders and sentenced to life imprisonment. Even though her motives have not been acceptably explained, and she was known to have suffered from mental illnesses, Falling was not classified as legally insane.

Chapter 12
The Unsolved Killings

Unfortunately, not all cases of serial killings are solved. It has already been shown that Black Widows and Angels of Death are able to evade apprehension for significant periods. Other times their identities remain unknown forever; their crimes are suddenly brought to a halt, either because the perpetrator died, or because the perpetrator was imprisoned for other felonies, or, for other unknown psychological factors. At any rate, the serial murders remain unsolved.

William Hodges Bingham and his family worked in Lancaster castle in England. After thirty years as a caretaker in a supervisory position, in 1911 Bingham died suddenly. Within a few weeks William Bingham's daughter, Margaret, was also found dead. Despite being in very good health, Margaret's brother also died shortly afterwards. An autopsy report was requested, and it was found that he had died from arsenic poisoning.

Because of the arsenic poisoning, a post-mortem examination was done on Bingham and his daughter. The report showed that they too had died from poisoning. The only surviving relative of the family, Edith Bingham, was accused of the three murders, but was soon acquitted as insufficient evidence could be found against her. As Edith would inherit the estate from her deceased relatives, it was commonly accepted that she was the killer; however, the case remained officially unsolved.

Females, the loving and caring protectors of our species and the ones that are more susceptible to danger, are in fact the most dangerous as they are the least suspected of the serial killers. Like their male counterparts, they show no remorse and have no mercy for their victims. Should we still call them the weaker sex? I think not.

Chapter 13
Gertrude Baniszewki

Gertrude Baniszewki

The Torture Mother

On October 26th, 1965, sixteen-year-old Sylvia Likens was found dead. A 911 call was received about a girl who had stopped breathing. When the police arrived at the house, Sylvia was found dead, lying on a mattress. She was half-naked, and lying on a bed soaked with urine. Her body bore scars, burns, and welts, and the words, *"I am a prostitute and proud of it,"* were engraved into her skin. The owner of the house was Gertrude Baniszewski. She claimed that Sylvia had been staying in the house during the summer with her sister, Jenny, and that she had brought the death and torture onto herself by running away. Baniszewski said that she was attacked by a pack of boys, and died shortly after returning home; however, Sylvia's sister Jenny had a different story to tell.

The actual story was that the Baniszewski had money problems. Gertrude had been trying to keep up the home and feed seven children at the same time. Her income consisted of working at the Indianapolis Motor Speedway selling soda pop, and small child support payments from her ex-husband.

Gertrude was given twenty dollars per week to watch the Likens children who were traveling with the Florida circus, and they had moved in with Baniszewski in July of 1965. When Sylvia and Jenny's parents were late with the first week's payment, Gertrude Baniszewski decided to give Sylvia and Jenny a beating, and while beating them she shouted, *"I took care of you bitches for nothing!"* Even though she was paid the next day, it did not bother Gertrude one bit. Her cruelty escalated over the next few months. The methods went from beatings by hand to paddles, belts, and even wooden boards, and she enforced harder punishment on Sylvia.

Baniszewski also recruited others to help her beat the children. Her first helpers were two of her own children. Then she even used some of the neighborhood children. One of them used her as a human punching bag, flinging her into concrete walls and down flights of stairs as a way to practice his martial arts throws. At Baniszewski's instruction, they even ground the glowing tips of cigarettes into Sylvia's flesh, inflicting over one hundred and fifty burns.

Sylvia urinated on the mattress one night, and the basement was made her prison. She was starved of food and forced to eat and drink her own feces and urine. Next, she was forced to insert a coke bottle in her vagina as a part of a bizarre strip tease. With a heated needle, Baniszewski proceeded to etch the words into Sylvia's belly. Sylvia died after being knocked down onto the concrete floor when she was trying to get the attention of the neighbors.

Gertrude was sentenced to life in prison for first-degree murder. As she was a model prisoner, however, she was up for parole in 1985. The news of Baniszewski's parole hearing sent shockwaves through the Indiana community. Jenny Likens and her family appeared on television to speak out against Baniszewski, as did members of two anti-crime groups, Protect the Innocent, and Society's League against Molestation. They travelled to Indiana to oppose her parole and support the Likens family and began a sidewalk picket campaign. Over the course of two months, the groups collected over forty thousand signatures from the citizens of Indiana demanding that Baniszewski be kept behind bars.

Despite efforts to keep her in prison, Baniszewski walked out December 4th, 1985, and traveled to Iowa where she later died from lung cancer in 1990 at the age of sixty.

Chapter 14
Margie Barfield

Marie Bullard was born on October 23rd, 1932, in Cumberland County, North Carolina, and is an American Serial Killer.

She claims she was molested by her father, starting when she was thirteen. The stories, however, are disputed by seven of her siblings who deny all charges of abuse in any form, by either parent, and it must be granted that Margie's early development seemed normal for the given time and place. She dropped out of high school in her junior year and then eloped with Thomas

Burke at the age of seventeen. Settling in Paxton, she bore two children.

The dilemma started after fifteen years of marriage when Thomas Burke's luck turned for the worst overnight. He was discharged from his job and consequently injured in a car crash. He then began to drink heavily in order to drown his sorrows. Marriage became a sort of warfare, with Margie hiding her husband's whiskey – sometimes she would pour it down the sink – and finally committing him to the Dorothea Dix Hospital, in Raleigh, as an alcoholic. She worked at a local mill to support the family and relied on prescription tranquilizers.

Thomas returned from the hospital sober and sullen, bitter at his wife's betrayal. In 1969, after he was burned to death in bed, authorities dismissed the death as accidental, caused by reckless smoking in bed. Later on, however, with the advantage of hindsight, there would be a dark thought of foul play.

Three years later, in 1971, Margie married Jennings Barfield. Only six months after getting married, he died suddenly, and his death was attributed to natural causes.

It would take seven years for the authorities to exhume and re-autopsy Barfield, revealing a lethal dose of arsenic in his system. By the time she murdered Barfield, Margie was dependent on prescription drugs, inaccurately mixing her pills, and as a result she was hospitalized four times for overdose. Although she was a drug addict, she maintained an active interest in religion and taught Sunday school at the local Pentecostal church on a regular basis.

Margie had another problem: she was always short on cash, so she started writing bad checks to cover her addiction. She appeared many times in court for this only to receive slaps on the wrists. She continued, however, and in 1974 forged her mother's name for a thousand dollar loan application. Panicking when she realized the bank might try to contact the real Lillie Bullard for verification, she decided to eliminate the problem by feeding her mother a lethal dose of insecticide. Yet again, the death was attributed to natural causes.

Two years later, Margie Barfield was employed by Dollie Edwards as a live-in house cleaner. As a fringe benefit, Dollie's nephew, Stuart Taylor, started dating Margie. Their relationship, however, did not stop the fearless Barfield from poisoning Dollie in February of 1977. Apparently, she had no motives, as there was not anything stolen, and the officials and doctor chalked it up to a sudden death of acute gastroenteritis.

A couple of months later, Barfield next moved in with John Lee, eighty, and his wife Record, seventy-six, to take care of them. "Heaven forbid." Again, with no motive, she started poisoning John Lee. Before his death, he lost sixty-five pounds. He died on June 4th, 1977. She then proceeded to poison Lee's widow, but gave up her job in October, leaving her frail survivor behind.

Moving right along to a Lumberton rest home, Barfield was twice caught forging checks on her boyfriend's, Stuart

Taylor's account. He forgave her each time, but they argued angrily after her third offense, on January 31st, 1978. That night, Margie spiked his beer with poison and kept up the dosage until Taylor died on February 4th. Relatives rejected the diagnosis of "acute gastroenteritis" and demanded a full autopsy, resulting in the discovery of arsenic. "Finally!"

While being interrogated, Margie Barfield confessed to the murders of Taylor, her mother, second husband, Dollie Edwards, and John Lee. A jury deliberated for less than an hour and convicted Barfield of first-degree murder. She was executed by lethal injection on November 2nd, 1984.

"I sometimes wonder how long it takes the authorities to add two and two together. Lovely lady wasn't she."

Chapter 15
Martha Beck and Raymond Fernandez

Martha Seabrook, born in 1920, was raped by her brother by the time she was thirteen. She had already grown prodigiously obese by that time. This horrible experience may explain her appetite for peculiar sex and her yearning for a life of romance. It may also have been at the root of her progressively callous outlook of other people. Martha was educated as a nurse and worked as an undertaker's assistant before being selected the superintendent of a home for crippled children at Pensacola, Florida.

Raymond Fernandez was six years older than Martha, born in Hawaii, but raised in Connecticut by his Spanish parents. They did live a spell in Spain where he had married and fathered four children, all of whom he had long since abandoned. He had served with the British Intelligence Service during World War II and in 1945 sustained a head injury, which disturbed an already not so stable personality.

He began studying black magic and claimed to have an overwhelming power over women. Whatever the reason, Fernandez was considered to have worked his way into more than a hundred women's hearts, homes, and bank accounts, over the next few years, draining them all dry. All the victims had been chosen from notices in a newspaper called the Lonely Hearts Clubs, where he eventually met up with Martha Beck, and together added murder to fraud and deception.

Martha placed demands on Raymond's faithfulness, going to excessive and often parody lengths to make sure that he did not accomplish any other lonely heart connections. One time, Martha demanded that she sleep with one of the victims herself to make sure there was no nighttime fun and games. Nevertheless, Fernandez found it difficult to control his lothario urges and often became the focal point of Martha's violent rage.

Fernandez met another woman, sixty-six-year-old, Janet Fay, from New York, and squandered her savings with the promise of marriage. He invited her to his apartment to meet his so-called sister, who happened to be Martha, where he then strangled and beat her to death. Only weeks after the disposal of Janet Fay, next up was Delphine Downing, a very young widow who had a two-year-old daughter. Fernandez did not waste any time and moved into Downing's house in Michigan, which really upset poor Martha. After stealing what money and possessions she had, the killing duo forced sleeping pills into Delphine and then shot her in the head. In order to stop the baby from crying, Martha Beck drowned her in the bathtub.

Neighbors of Delphine and Rainelle Downing reported them missing. Eventually they were found buried in the cellar under newly poured cement. The neighbors told police she had a live-in boyfriend, and police immediately obtained an arrest warrant as a person of interest.

Because Michigan does not have the death penalty, once Beck and Fernandez were caught, they were extradited to New York for the murders, where they confessed to the Downing and Fay killings, but denied the other seventeen deaths they were suspected of causing. The Lonely Hearts Killers were found guilty of three murders and subsequently sentenced to death. Old Sparky fried both of them on March 8th, 1951 at Sing Sing prison in New York City.

Apparently, the last words of Fernandez were: *"I wanna shout it out, I love Martha! What do the public know about love?"* - Raymond Fernandez.

Chapter 16
Lizzie Borden

The Lizzie Borden case has bewildered and mesmerized people who are interested in true crime for many decades. Very few cases in American history have attracted as much attention as the hatchet murders of her parents, Andrew and Abby Borden. Despite the horrific nature of the crimes, the unexpected temperament of the accused was not that of a hatchet maniac, but that of a churchgoing Sunday school teacher who was highly regarded.

The accused was eventually found not guilty for the violent and bloody murders of two people due to unusual circumstances. It was an era of swift justice and vast newspaper coverage. And as evidence against her was almost entirely contingent, and the prosecution considered incompetent, public opinion was divided to the guilt or innocence of Lizzie.

Lizzie Borden lived her life where she was born in Fall River, Massachusetts. Lizzie's mother, Sarah, died when Lizzie was less than three years old. Lizzie had another sister, Emma, who was nine years older than she. Her father, Andrew, remarried to Abby Gray and lived a quiet and uneventful life. Until 1892. That year, Lizzie was active at church, including teaching Sunday school and a being member of the Women's Christian Temperance Union (WCTU). In 1890, Lizzie Borden traveled abroad briefly with some friends.

Andrew Borden became somewhat wealthy, and was notoriously tight with his money. In 1884, when Andrew presented his wife's half-sister a house, his daughters

Lizzie and Emma objected and fought with their stepmother, Abby, refusing after that to call her "mother," and started simply calling her "Mrs. Borden." Andrew tried to make harmony with his daughters, giving them some funds, and allowed them to rent out his old family home.

In early August of 1892, Andrew and Abby became ill and had an attack of vomiting. Abby Borden told a friend that she suspected poisoning. Lizzie's uncle came to stay at the house, and on August 4th, her uncle and father went into town together. Andrew returned alone and lay down in the family room. The house cleaner, who had earlier been ironing and washing windows, was taking a nap when Lizzie called to her to come downstairs. Lizzie said that her father had been killed in the barn. He had been hacked in the face and head with an axe or hatchet. Shortly after, Abby was also found dead in a bedroom, also hacked many times with an axe or hatchet. Later tests showed that Abby had died one to two hours before Andrew.

As Andrew had died without a will,

this meant that his estate, worth between $300,000 and $500,000, would go to his daughters, Lizzie and Emma, and not to Abby's heirs.

As she was the only one with a motive, and her sister was away, Lizzie Borden was arrested.

Evidence included a report that she had tried to burn her dress one week after the murder, and reports that she had attempted to buy poison just before the murders. The murder weapon was never found; however, a hatchet head that may have been washed and intentionally made to look dirty was found in the cellar.

Lizzie's trial, commencing on June 3rd 1893, was covered by local and national news. Lizzie did not testify, having told the inquisition that she had been searching the barn for fishing equipment and then eating pears outside during the time of the murders. She said, *"I am innocent. I leave it to my counsel to speak for me."*

The jury was not convinced that Lizzie had killed her father and stepmother as there was not any direct evidence and therefore acquitted her on June 20th, 1893. Emma had returned and they bought a big house that they called, Maplecroft, and Lizie took to calling her herself Lizbeth instead of Lizzie.

Lizzie Borden died at Fall River, Massachusetts, in 1927, and was buried next to her father and stepmother.

"They certainly didn't have the technology back a hundred years ago to ascertain the certainty whether Lizzie Borden really did kill Andrew and Abby Borden. I guess it will remain a mystery."

Chapter 17
Judias Buenoano

Judy Welty was born on April 4th, 1943, in Quanah, Texas, the daughter of a wandering farm worker. She hardly knew her mother but in later years would describe her as a full-blooded member of the Mesquite Apache tribe, which never existed. Judias was named after her mother who had died of tuberculosis when her young daughter was barely two years old. The family was split up and Judias and her baby brother, Robert, were sent to live with their grandparents while the two older siblings were placed for adoption.

Welty had re-united with her father and had been the target of abuse by both parents (her father had remarried). She was burned, beaten, sometimes starved, and demanded to work as a slave in the house. When she was fourteen years old she spent sixty days in the local lockup after scalding two of her stepbrothers with grease and attacking both parents with fists and thrown objects. While in jail, she was held with adult prostitutes, and when asked if she wanted to go home by the Judge, she instead chose to go to reform school. She despised her family and stayed away from them.

Working under the name of Anna Schultz, Judy returned to Roswell and worked as a nurse's aide. A year later, she gave birth to an illegitimate son, Michael. In 1962, she married James Goodyear, an air force officer, and four years later they had a son, James Junior. They moved to Orlando Florida and shortly thereafter her husband left on a tour of duty in Vietnam.

Three months after returning from his tour, Goodyear suddenly grew sick and died from an identified illness. Five days later, Judy cashed in three life insurance policies on her husband. Two months later, their home burned down and she was awarded $90,000 in insurance. Shortly after, she moved her kids to Pensacola, Florida, and met up with Bobby Morris. He moved to Colorado in 1977 and took Judy and her kids with her. Prior to leaving Pensacola, however, she had another fire in her second home, and again collected insurance.

On January 4th, 1978, Bobby Joe Morris was admitted to San Rafael Hospital. Doctors could find no cause for his sudden illness and he was released to Judy's care two weeks later. Just two days after being released from hospital, he collapsed at the dinner table and was rushed back to the hospital where he died on January 28th. His death certificate officially declared that he'd had a cardiac arrest and metabolic acidosis.

Authors Note: Is it just me, or is did Judy have the worst luck? hmmm.

In early February, Judy cashed in

three more life insurance policies, this time for the death of Morris, and her bank account was doing quite well. Backing up a few years, in 1974, Bobby and Judy had visited his hometown of Brewton in Alabama. At the time, a male resident was found dead in a motel after being shot in the chest and having his throat cut. Bobby's mother had overheard Judy telling him that, "The son of a bitch shouldn't have come up here in the first place. He knew if he came up here he was gonna die." So when Bobby's family heard that he'd suddenly died, they suspected murder right away.

Just three months after Bobby Morris had died, Judy legally changed her last name and that of her children to Buenoano, an apparent tribute to her late husband and imaginary Apache mother. A month after that she moved her family back in Pensacola, settling into a home in Gulf Breeze.

Michael Jr. continued his pattern of academic failure, dropping out of high school in his sophomore year. He joined the army in June of 1979, drawing an assignment to Fort Benning in Georgia, after basic training. En route to his new post, he stopped off to visit his mother in Florida, and that was the beginning of the end. When he reached Fort Benning on November 6th, he was already showing symptoms of base metal poisoning. Army physicians found seven times the normal level of arsenic in Michael's body, and there was little they could do to reverse its critical action. After six weeks of care, the muscles of his arms and lower legs had withered to the point where Michael could neither walk nor use his hands. He left the hospital wearing braces and a prosthetic device on one arm.

In another turn of events, this one fatal yet again, in May of 1980, Michael, his younger brother, and mother, were canoeing near Milton, Florida, when their boat upturned. James and Judy made it safely to shore; however, Michael was not so lucky and drowned. Judy, in press reports of the incident, referred to herself as Dr. Judias Buenoano, a physician in Fort Walton. The local authorities acknowledged her explanation of the accident and closed their files.

However, the army investigators were unrelenting, launching their own investigation for verification on May 27th, 1980. Just four months later, Michael's military life insurance was paid, amounting to $20,000. Upon discovering that there were two other private life insurance policies outside of the military, the sheriff's officers began to look at the case more closely. While doing so, and after consulting with handwriting experts, they revealed that the two civilian policies on Michael's life might have been forged. They proceeded to investigate without Judy's knowledge at this point.

Meanwhile, Judy did not waste time in searching for another victim, er, man. She met up with John Gentry II, a businessman in Pensacola, Florida. She told him that she had a Ph.D. in Biochemistry and another Ph.D. in Psychology from the University of Alabama. It was all BS, however. But Gentry accepted it and indulged her with expensive gifts and cruises.

John and Judias (she liked to be called Judias as she was a doctor and all), bought private life insurance policies on each other in October of 1982 which was supposed to be $50,000 coverage each. However, without John knowing, Judias later increased the payout amount to $500,000, and paid the premiums herself.

Judias started poisoning Gentry just two months later, giving him victim, er, vitamin pills, which caused him to become ill; subsequently, he was admitted to hospital for twelve days. Gentry noticed that his symptoms subsided after he stopped taking vitamins, but had no reason to be suspicious of his wife. For whatever reason, she decided that poisoning him was not going to work.

Well, there is more than one way to skin a cat. John Gentry was at a party on June 25th, 1983, and left early to celebrate, as Judias had told him that she was pregnant. Gentry left the party and planned to pick up champagne to take home with him. However, when he turned the key in the ignition of his car, a bomb exploded.

Luckily for him, not so lucky for her, his life was saved by the O.R. surgeons.

Due to the nature of a car bombing, an obvious attempt at murder, the police began investigating and, upon questioning John Gentry on June 29th, learned that the insurance policy which he claimed was for $50,000 was actually for $500,000. During their investigation, the police also learned – after conducting a background check on Judias – that she was not a doctor; nor did she have any Ph.D's; and on top of that she'd been surgically sterilized way back in 1975. John was shocked to discover all of the lies she had told him, and he had had enough.

Wondering what else she'd lied about or done, John gave the police several of the vitamin pills that Judias had been giving him back in 1982. Examination of these pills showed that they contained Para formaldehyde, a poison with no known medical uses. However, the prosecution office in Florida declined to file charges of attempted murder for lack of sufficient evidence, but they later obtained a warrant to search her home.

On July 27th, one month after the car explosion, court officers, federal agents, and police, searched Judias' home in Gulf Breeze where they collected tape and wire from her bedroom that appeared to match components that had been used in the car bomb device. With further investigating, they linked Judias by way of phone records to the source where she purchased the dynamite in Alabama. She was arrested and charged with attempted murder. Lo and behold, she was released on bail.

The investigation continued before her trial, meanwhile, and on January 14th, 1984, Judias was indicted for one count of murder in the death of her son, with a supplementary count of grand theft for the insurance frauds. Upon her arrest that evening, she had a dramatic fit of convulsions and wound up in Santa Rosa Hospital under security.

Once the authorities got started, they dug through Judias' past and uncovered all sorts of mischief. Bobby Joe Morris' body was exhumed on February 11th, and further testing revealed arsenic in his remains. Judias was sentenced to life without parole for the first twenty-five years, but it did not stop there for the investigators. In Florida, in July, just a short few weeks after being sentenced, authorities exhumed the body of her late boyfriend, one Gerald Dossett. Unfortunately, there were no signs of arsenic and therefore no charged filed in that particular case. The body of James Goodyear was also then disinterred on March 14th, which showed results of arsenic poisoning.

Judy went to trial for the murder of husband James Goodyear. A week was devoted to the trial, with Judy denying any criminal activity. The jurors, however, weren't buying into her act, and convicted her yet again of first-degree murder, sentencing her to die by electrocution on March 30th, 1998 at 7 a.m.

Early Monday morning on March 30th, Judy showered and was dressed by female correctional officers. Her head was shaved to ensure a good electrical conduit – and so that her hair did not catch fire during the electrocution. She entered the execution chamber at 7 a.m. accompanied by several guards. She was strapped into the large oak chair at her wrists, waist, chest, and legs. When asked if she had a final comment, she replied "No sir," and kept her eyes shut tight. A leather mask was placed over her head, covering her face and, at the signal from the warden, the automatic electrocution cycle commenced at 7:08 a.m. She was pronounced dead at 7:13 a.m.

Chapter 18
Christine Falling

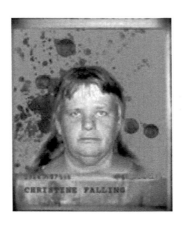

Christine Falling was born to a poor family on March 12, 1963, in Perry, Florida. She was considered obese and slow. In order to control her epileptic seizures, she needed regular doses of medication. At a very early age, she was known to drop cats from deadly heights to *"test their nine lives."* As a way of showing affection to the cats, she would strangle them. This was all before the age of nine, at which time Christine and her sister were placed in a children's shelter in Orlando, Florida, for a year.

At the young age of only fourteen, Falling married a man who was in his twenties, and their marriage lasted just six weeks. The couple would fight violently, and Falling would often throw things at her husband, including, once, a twenty-five pound stereo. Upon splitting up, she visited the hospital constantly – upwards of 50 times – complaining of vaginal bleeding, snakebites, etc., and the doctors found nothing to treat. It was quite evident that she was going through a hypochondriac stage.

Christine would babysit for family and neighbors in order to make money. On February 25th, she was babysitting Cassidy Johnson, aged two, who had to be taken to the hospital where she was diagnosed with encephalitis, and died just three days later. The autopsy, however, revealed that the cause of death was blunt force trauma to the head. When asked, Christine said that the baby had passed out and fallen out of her crib, but the doctor did not believe her story and contacted the police to investigate. The note to the police, however, somehow got lost; the incident was not looked into, and the parents were not apprised of the coroner's report.

Shortly after that incident, Falling moved to Lakeland, Florida and another job babysitting when, all of a sudden, four-year-old Jeffrey Davis stopped breathing while in her care. The autopsy conducted showed symptoms of myocarditis, a heart problem which is seldom critical. While the family of little Jeffrey was attending his funeral, Christine was hired to babysit two year old Joseph Spring, Jeffrey Davis's cousin. While at the funeral for Jeffrey, little Joseph died suddenly that afternoon in his crib, apparently while taking a nap. The physician's indicated there was a viral infection that may have killed little Joseph, and noted that it was quite possible for the same virus to have killed Jeffrey too.

"It's hard to believe the connections were not made at this point in my opinion."

William Swindle, seventy-seven, died in his kitchen in July of 1981 on his caretaker's first day on the job. You guessed it: Christine Falling had switched from babysitting to housekeeping. A short while after that, Christine and her stepsister took her eight-month-old niece for a standard vaccination. After leaving the doctor's office, the stepsister ran into the store, leaving Christine alone with the baby. When she came back to the car, the little eight month old had stopped breathing.

It was not until July 2nd, 1982, when little ten week old Travis Coleman was smothered that the police began to pay attention. The autopsy report on Coleman showed internal ruptures caused by suffocation. Immediately following the autopsy report, Falling was taken for questioning where she admitted to killing three babies by, in her words, *"smotheration."*

"The way I done it, I seen it done on TV show," she explained. *"I had my own way, though, simple and easy. No one would hear them scream."*

Christine Falling was given a life sentence with no chance of parole possible for twenty-five years.

Chapter 19
Caril Ann Fugate
and
Charles Starkweather

Charles Starkweather, known as "Chuck" or "Charlie" to his friends and family, was born in 1938. Caril Ann Fugate was born in 1943. At the age of fourteen, in 1956, she was in love with Charlie who was five years her senior.

Starkweather had a speech impediment and was often made fun of in school, getting into many fights. He did not do well in school, but excelled in gym where he released his pent-up rage and frustration. He dropped out of high school in his senior year and went to work in a newspaper warehouse, which he later quit to work as a garbage collector and used his route to plan robberies. His first robbery was at the Crest Service Station in Lincoln on December 1st, 1957, where he held Robert Colvert, twenty-one, at gunpoint, robbed him of $100, abducted him, and then took him to a secluded location where he shot him in the head.

In 1958, the massacres commenced. It was on January 21st, 1958, that Caril Ann returned from school to her family's one story house in the poor Belmont section of Lincoln, Nebraska. Apparently, after an argument with Starkweather, Marion Bartlett, fifty-seven, Caril's father, and her mother, Velda Bartlett, thirty-six, were shot in the head. Betty Jean, Caril's two and a half years old sister, was strangled and stabbed to death in her bed. Following the murders, the couple simply made sandwiches and had lunch together.

Starkweather and Fugate hid the bodies in various locations behind the house and the young couple lived in the house for days. Twice, relatives came by to find out why nobody from the family had been seen. Caril sent them away at the door, telling them everyone was sick. She taped a note on the door reading, *"Stay a Way Every Body is sick with the Flue."* Caril Ann's grandmother felt something was suspicious and contacted the police, but when they arrived on January 27th, the couple was gone.

A search turned up the body of Marion wrapped in paper in the chicken house. Caril's mother, Velda, and baby Betty Jean were found in an outbuilding. The lovers were already driving across Nebraska killing and stealing. What the authorities did not know was that just four hours earlier the couple had driven to a Highway 77 service station to buy gas, a box of .410 shotgun shells, and two boxes of .225, before heading to the rural farmlands of Bennet, just sixteen miles southeast of

Lincoln. Starkweather knew where they could hide out for a while in a farmhouse owned by seventy year-old August Meyer, who often invited the Starkweather family to hunt on his property.

On their way to the Meyers farmhouse, their car became stuck in the mud. Robert Jensen, seventeen, and his date, Carol King, sixteen, were driving by at the time and offered to help. Starkweather instantly shot them in the head with his .22 rifle and made a failed attempt to rape King before stuffing their bodies into an abandoned storm cellar. They continued on to the Meyer's farm with the intention of obtaining more guns and ammunition. Upon arriving, Starkweather killed August Meyers with a .410-gauge shotgun and placed his body in a washhouse before heading back to Lincoln.

After leaving the Meyer's farm, Starkweather and Fugate drove to the house of industrialist C. Lauer Ward and his wife, Clara. After entering, Clara and their house cleaner, Lillian Fencl were fatally stabbed to death. Starkweather even snapped the neck of their family dog. When Mr. Ward returned home that evening, Starkweather shot and killed him. The killing sick duo filled the Ward's 1956 Packard with stolen jewelry from the house and fled to Nebraska.

The murders of Mr. and Mrs. Ward, and Lillian Fencl, created an upheaval within Lancaster County. All law enforcement agencies in the county conducted a house-by-house search for the killers. Sheriff Merle Karnopp deputized and armed over one hundred men. Governor Victor Anderson contacted the Nebraska National Guard. Schools closed, kids stayed indoors, the National Bank was secured, and in total, over twelve hundred officers were searching for the killers.

A traveling shoe salesperson named Merle Collison, thirty-seven, pulled his Buick off Highway 87 to take a nap. While he was asleep, Caril climbed into the back seat and opened the door for Charlie who shot Merle Collison nine times in the head. Joe Sprinkle, a geologist, saw something going on in a car, and stopped to see if someone needed help. Starkweather instantly pointed a gun at his head just as Deputy Sheriff William Romer came by. Sprinkle ran to the Deputy yelling, *"it's Starkweather, he's going to kill me."* Charlie hopped into Sprinkle's car and rammed a roadblock until a police bullet shattered his windshield. Starkweather, covered in blood from flying glass, immediately surrendered.

Charlie and Caril were arrested and locked up in a Wyoming jail until their arraignment on March 26th, 1958. Starkweather pleaded not guilty so there would be a trial. Caril Fugate also pleaded that she was not guilty.

Charlie Starkweather's trial began on May 5th, 1958, in Lancaster District Court, and ended seventeen days later on May 23rd when a jury found him guilty and gave him the death penalty. He was executed by electrocution in the Nebraska State Prison on June 25th, 1959.

In the meantime, Caril Fugate's trial started on October 27th, 1958. Throughout her trial, Caril insisted she was held hostage and feared for her life. Before Starkweather was executed, he was brought to Caril's trial from his death cell to testify that she was a keen participant and could have escaped when he left her alone with loaded guns.

On November 21st, after only ten hours of deliberation, the five woman and seven man jury gave her a sentence of life in prison and she was sent to the Nebraska Correctional Center for Women in York.

An interesting note to make here is that Caril Fugate was allowed to complete her high school education at the Nebraska Center for Women. She read over 1,000 books, learned to sew, write, and ran a column in the prison paper. She was even allowed to partake in programs such as bowling, swimming, and shopping the town.

Further to this note, I will add that, on June 20th, 1976, killer Caril Fugate was released from prison as she was considered a model inmate. On September 28th, 1981, she was completed discharged by the parole board. She has never discussed her case in public since being released.

Chapter 20
Delfina and Maria
de Jesus Gonzalez

Delfina and Maria were two sisters from the Mexican City of Guanajuato who operated the Rancho El Angel, a brothel, from the mid 1950s to mid 1960s. They recruited prostitutes, got them addicted to drugs, and forced them to serve the wicked and humiliating needs of their clientele.

When a girl became too ill, such as by being injured by repeat rape, or even as little as having lost their "prettiness," they would be killed. They were known to kill any visitors who had large amounts of cash.

On suspicion of kidnapping young girls in the Guanajuato area, the police picked up a woman named Josefina Gutiérrez, a procuress, and it is believed that she gave up the sisters. Upon searching the compound, police officers found the bodies of eleven males, eighty women and many fetuses, a total of ninety-one.

Investigations exposed that they would recruit prostitutes through help-wanted ads and then force them to work. The Gonzalez sisters were each sentenced to forty years in prison in 1964.

In prison, Delfina died due to an accident. Maria finished her sentence and dropped out of sight after her release. Although they are often cited as the killers, there were also two other sisters who helped in their crimes, Carmen and Maria Luisa. Carmen died in jail due to cancer. Maria Luisa went mad because she feared that she would be killed by angry protesters.

"As this happened almost fifty years

ago and in a foreign country, it is unbelievably hard to obtain information about the crimes, considering almost 100 people were killed."

Chapter 21
Karla Homolka
and
Paul Bernardo

Karla Homolka, the eldest of three daughters, was born on May 4th, 1970 in St. Catharines, Ontario, Canada, to Karel and Dorothy Homolka. Paul Bernardo was born on August 27th, 1964 in Toronto, Ontario, Canada, to Marilyn and Kenneth Bernardo. Paul and Karla met in 1987 and married in 1991. Shortly after they married, it was all downhill from there. Author Note: I am not proud to say that this lovely couple is from my country.

Before they started their team rape and killings in 1991, Bernardo already had quite the history of rape, although he was not known to the authorities at that time. Between May 1987 and July 1990, he had raped eighteen young girls between the ages of fifteen and twenty-two.

His first murder victim was Tammy Homolka, Karla's younger sister. Bernardo encouraged Karla to drug her sister. When she did, Bernardo raped her before she woke up. Several months later they drugged Tammy again and both of them raped her, but this time Tammy died after choking on her own vomit. The police ruled it an accidental death, not knowing that before they called 911, Bernardo and Homolka had redressed Tammy and removed any incriminating evidence. Tammy Homolka died at the tender age of fifteen on December 23rd, 1990.

Meet Leslie Mahaffy, a young girl, only fifteen, born on July 5th, 1976, and murdered on June 16th, 1991. Two day before her death, Leslie went out for an evening with a few friends. Her curfew was 10 p.m. as the Scarborough rapist was active and like many parents, Leslie's were afraid. Unfortunately, Leslie was having fun with the girls and ignored the ground rules set up by her parents. Her parents anticipated that she would break curfew and decided to teach her a lesson which they would forever regret. Leslie arrived home after 2 a.m. to find herself locked out of the house. She did not know what to do so she called a friend to see if she could stay over, but her friend's mom told her to go home and face the consequences.

Bernardo was crouched behind a car when Leslie came strolling by. Carrying a hunting knife, he forced her into his car and drove her to his house where he undressed her, blindfolded her, and videotaped her naked. He was going to have vaginal intercourse with Leslie but he ejaculated prematurely. When Karla woke up, he gave her instructions on how he wanted her to have sex with Leslie while he videotaped. This done, he instructed the submissive

Karla to film him while he sodomized Leslie.

The brute power of his anal penetration caused Leslie to cry hysterically. After twenty-four hours of disgusting rape and torture, the couple killed Leslie and, later that night, Bernardo used a circular saw to dismember her body and place her in cement.

On June 29th, 1991, a couple enjoying canoeing trip on Lake Gibson spotted a concrete block in the water. The cement block had what looked like animal flesh coming out of the cracks. There were anglers on the bank; they were asked to help retrieve the cement block. After splitting it with a crowbar, they were devastated when they saw a foot and the calf of a human crawling with maggots.

Enter Kristen French, born May 10th, 1976, a beautiful fifteen year old young girl. On April 16th, 1992, one month shy of her 16th birthday, she was walking home from school when Homolka lured her over to her car on the pretense of asking for directions. As Kristen was giving directions on the map, Bernardo, brandishing a knife, attacked her from behind and forced her into the car.

This hostage-taking was observed by several witnesses. A BOLO was sent out to all units and a sketch was prepared of Bernardo by a witness. Kristen was kept for three days, being raped and tortured while the couple videotaped it all, and was forced to drink large quantities of alcohol before she was killed by Bernardo and Homolka. She was found in a ditch on April 30th, but as she was not dismembered, the investigators did not believe it was the same person who had killed Leslie Mahaffy.

The Green Ribbon Task Force was set up by the police with Superintendent Vincent Bevan taking the lead. The F.B.I. in the U.S. was consulted in an effort to profile the rapist. Citizens were concerned and kept their children at home. In the meantime, after the death of Kristen French, the newlywed-killing-duet moved to the Niagara Falls area.

As the drawing sketch of the rapist was plastered on TV, in post offices, in stores, and sidewalks, the police received calls saying that the man they were looking for resembled a man named Paul Bernardo.

The investigators went to Bernardo's home where he claimed he was not the rapist/killer but admitted that, yes, the picture did resemble him, which he said was embarrassing.

While the detectives were there, they noted that the car in the driveway looked nothing like the Capri which witnesses had seen, but instead was a Nissan. Paul Bernardo, therefore, was not considered a suspect. Police were no further ahead and Bernardo continued his spree of rape and murder of teenage girls.

By February, 1993, Bernardo made a mistake that would put him in the limelight as a suspect. After he blackened both eyes of Homolka and knocked out several of her teeth, she called 911. The police in Niagara Falls took her to the hospital and began investigating the matter. Karla was admitted to hospital and her uncle came to visit her. She whispered to him that Bernardo had killed Leslie Mahaffy and Kristen French and went on to tell her uncle that he was indeed the Scarborough Rapist.

Author's Note: she never mentioned about the death of her sister Tammy. Homolka hired lawyer, George Walker, and told him that she wanted immunity if she gave up Bernardo. Walker said he would see what he could do.

The next day, on February 11th, 1993, Homolka's lawyer, George Walker, met with Director, Murray Segal, of the Crown Criminal Law Office. Walker told Segal that they had videotapes of the rapes, and Segal advised Walker that, considering Homolka's involvement in the crimes, full immunity was unlikely.

Paul was arrested and charged with the murders of Mahaffy and French and the rapes of several young girls. It was not until the 19th of February that police were granted a warrant to search Benardo's and Homolka's house. They did not, however, find any videotapes as Homolka had claimed. They did find a complete register in Bernardo's handwriting of all the murders and rapes, as well as books on serial killers, and perverted sex magazines. The much-wanted videotapes were in the possession of Bernardo's lawyer who surrendered them when he withdrew from the case.

Before the tapes were handed to the police, a plea bargain was arranged based on Homolka's testimony. She would receive twelve years for each of the two victims (not her sister). The prosecutor said that it had to be done in order to nail Bernardo. Her earliest release date would be June, 2001. Once the videotapes were obtained from Bernardo's lawyer, it clearly showed that Homolka was heavily involved in cruel sex acts with both of the girls. Her lawyer could see for himself that she was a willing and eager participant in the crimes. As this news broke, public outraged for her plea bargain grew. The media dubbed it the worst deal the Canadian government had ever made with a criminal witness.

Bernardo's trial started in May of 1995. He was charged with two counts of murder in the 1st degree, two counts of aggravated sexual assault, two counts of kidnapping, two counts of forcible confinement, and one count of dismembering a body. He pleaded not guilty.

The prosecutor, Ray Houlahan, first rolled a tape of Homolka, naked and masturbating with a flashlight inside her. The jury was disgusted. They knew there would be pornography, but they hadn't thought it would be so explicit. The prosecutor's intention, however, was to show the court how Bernardo forced women to do anything for him, even kill a sibling. A pin drop could be heard in court when Homolka testified, showing how they had drugged and raped her sister Tammy in order to demonstrate how terrified she was of Bernardo's violence and control.

Homolka was asked why she committed these horrifying crimes. She explained "Paul was very upset when he discovered she was not a virgin the first time they had sex. It was therefore, her responsibility to make it possible for him to take the virginity of her pretty younger sister Tammy. It would have to be videotaped without Tammy's knowing anything about it so I decided to give her to Paul as a Christmas present." This was the first time that the Homolka parents ever heard the details surrounding what had happened to their fifteen-year-old daughter, Tammy. They could not believe what they were hearing.

In the end, Bernardo got a life sentence and was classified as a dangerous offender, meaning he would never get out of prison. Bernardo is currently serving his term at the maximum-security prison in Quebec after being transferred early 2013 from the Kingston Penitentiary in Ontario. He remains in the segregation unit. He spends twenty-three hours every day in a four by eight-prison cell.

Homolka was released from prison in June of 2005. Since her release, she's remarried and now goes by the name, Emily Bordelais, and is awaiting a pardon. There is a Cause set up petitioning to stop her from obtaining this pardon. The website is: http://www.causes.com/causes/475014-stop-karla-homolka-from-getting-a-pardon

Chapter 22
Dorothea Puente

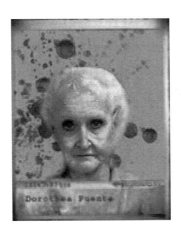

Dorothea Puente was born on January 9th, 1929, in Bernardino County, California. In 1945, she married a soldier named Fred McFaul who had just returned from the war. Their marriage, though, only last three years. Puente became desperate for money and started forging checks which landed her in jail for six months.

Puente got pregnant just after being released, but gave the baby up for adoption. In 1952, she again married, and this time the marriage lasted for fourteen years. She had a few scrapes with the law in the 60s, operating a brothel and being arrested for vagrancy. She divorced her husband of fourteen years and married Robert Puente, who was nineteen years her junior. That marriage lasted but two years.

In 1981, Puente started renting a boarding home with her friend Ruth Monroe. There, the murdering began. They went into business together attending to the elderly and mentally handicapped people. After a short time in business together, Ruth Monroe died suddenly and her death was ruled a suicide by the police. Apparently, the cause was an overdose of Codeine and Tylenol.

Just four weeks later, Puente was arrested and subsequently sent to prison for five years after a seventy-four-year-old man claimed she was drugging and stealing from him. She served only a few years for good behavior. While she was in jail, she had a pen pal, Everson Gillmouth, seventy-seven, who picked her up after her release. They planned to marry, and rented an apartment on F Street in Sacramento, California.

Once they were settled in their new place, a repairperson named Ismael Florez was hired by Puente in November of 1985 to do some woodwork for her. For his efforts, she gave him Gillmouth's 1980 Ford pickup as well as $800 cash. She hired Florez build her a box, allegedly to store papers and books, and instructed him to make it two feet by three feet by six feet long.

Once it was built and she had it filled and nailed shut, she asked her repairperson to help bring it to a storage depot. On the way, however, she told him to stop in Sutter County and dump the box on the riverbank in an unofficial household dumping site. Florez had assumed she wanted to keep the contents – that is why she had him build it – but Puente told him the contents of the box were just junk.

It was not until New Years Day, 1986 when the box and body within was discovered. The body of an elderly man was so decomposed that, according to the police, they could not identify him. It would be another three years before the body of Everson Gillmouth would be identified. Even in death, the pension checks would continue being cashed by Puente.

Puente continued looking after elderly residents, intercepting their mail, cashing their checks, and pocketing a good portion of them. In total, she took in another forty boarders after killing Gillmouth. She had her repairperson cover the basement with a cement slab and had the garage torn down and replaced with another cement slab. Shortly after he did all of this, he too disappeared.

When Alvaro Montoya was reported missing by his family on November 11th, 1988, the police went to the boarding house to have a look around. Upon searching the property, they found former tenant Leona Carpenter, seventy-eight, along with seven other bodies buried in the basement and even the flower garden.

Puente was charged and convicted of only three of the murders, as the prosecution could not produce enough evidence to secure convictions for all the murders. She was given two life sentences without parole for her crimes of murder.

On March 27th, 2011, Dorothea Puente, eighty-two, died in prison at the age from natural causes.

Chapter 23
Marybeth Tinning

The Baby Killer

Marybeth Roe was born on September 11th, 1942 in Duanesburg, New York. She was a normal student during school; however, on several occasions she attempted suicide as a cry for attention. After completing school, she worked menial jobs, but eventually became a nursing assistant at Ellis Hospital in Schenectady, New York.

She met Joe Tinning in 1963 and the

couple was married two years later. Together they had three children: Barbara, Joseph, and the youngest, Jennifer, who was sick at birth and died only a few weeks later of meningitis.

Three weeks later on January 20th, 1972, Marybeth took Joseph, aged two, to the Ellis Hospital emergency room after he'd had an apparent seizure. He was kept in the hospital for observation, but the doctors couldn't find anything wrong with him, and he was sent home. Only hours later, Joseph was back to the ER, but this time he died. Tinning told the doctors that she'd placed him in bed to sleep, and when she went back to check on him, he was blue, and tangled in the bed sheets. This was accepted by the hospital as accidental.

Not six weeks later, the mother was back in the E.R. with her four-year-old daughter, Barbara. The mother claimed the girl had gone into convulsions. She was checked out and advised to stay overnight. Tinning, however, wanted to take her home and, you guessed it, just hours later Tinning brought the girl back into the E.R..

Unconscious at the time, she later died. The medical doctor attributed Barbara's death to Reyes Syndrome. Within three months of each other, all three of the Tinning children had died.

Authors Note: How can one mother have such rotten luck?

Break out the champagne. Marybeth Tinning got pregnant again and in 1973, on Thanksgiving Day, gave birth to a baby boy, Timothy. Three weeks later Timothy was found dead in his crib. The doctors listed it as S.I.D.S., or sudden infant death syndrome.

Nathan Tinning was born two years later on March, 30th, 1975, the fifth child born to the couple. When Nathan was only five months old, Marybeth arrived at the Hospital with him dead in her arms. She claimed that she was driving and noticed that the baby was not breathing and rushed to the E.R. Once again, no foul play was suspected and no explanation was given for the child's death. The Tinnings decided to adopt in 1978, but before the adoption went through Tinning became pregnant again. So, in August, they adopted young Michael who was just a baby, and in October their 6th child, Mary Frances, was born.

When Mary Frances was only four months old, she supposedly had a seizure and was taken to the hospital. Unfortunately, the doctors were unable to save her and she died on February 20th. Nothing suspect was reported by the hospital or anyone. Marybeth Tinning then got pregnant again, and on November 19th Jonathan was born.

Authors Note: Isn't this getting repetitive?

Marybeth Tinning arrived at St. Clare's hospital with Jonathan on March 4th, 1980. Jonathan was unconscious, but was revived. Due to the family history of misfortune and babies dying, Jonathan was sent to Boston Hospital where he was thoroughly examined. The doctors could find no valid medical reason why the baby had simply stopped breathing. Jonathan returned home only to be brought back to the hospital three days later, dead, on March 24th.

The adopted child, Michael, was now two and a half years old, and on March 2nd of the following year, was carried into his pediatrician's office wrapped in a blanket, unconscious. Tinning calmly claimed that she could not wake the child, and when the doctor examined him, discovered he was already dead. It was previously believed that there was a genetic origin for the deaths of all the infants, but when their adopted child died too, someone finally took notice.

The police were called in to investigate and found that Tinning had been present every time a child had died. After interrogating her, she confessed to smothering them, and received twenty years to life in prison for the deaths of eight babies.

She is now living at the Bedford Hills Prison for Women in New York, serving out her twenty-year sentence. She had parole hearings in 2007, 2009, and 2011. Each time she was denied parole. Her latest hearing was January 20, 2013 and again she was denied parole.

Chapter 24

Rosemary
and
Fred West

Rosemary Letts was born on November 29th, 1953 in Devon, England. Frederick West was born on September 29th, 1941 in Herefordshire, England.

Rosemary and Fred were married on January 29th, 1972 and their daughter Mae was born on June 1st. To make money, Fred encouraged his wife to become a prostitute and she had seven children, three of mixed race. Both Rosemary and Fred came from families of incest and on many occasions, her father, Bill Letts, would visit their house to have sex with his daughter.

As they had many children, they hired Caroline Roberts, seventeen, as a nanny. Rosemary had set up a room in the house for her prostitution and called it "Rose's Room." To offset any suspicion about all the men coming and going, they told the nanny that she was a masseuse.

Caroline rejected sexual advances from both Rosemary and Fred. She left the house but was brought back, tied up, and raped by the couple. They threatened to lock her in the cellar and let black male customers have their way with her if she did not behave. Fred told her that they had killed hundreds of young girls and that their bodies had never been found.

Realizing they would kill her, Caroline gave in to them sexually without a fight. The next day, she reported the rape to the police, but withdrew her accusation when the case came to court; however, for a reduced charge and a fine of only fifty pounds, the Wetts' pleaded guilty.

Fred began raping his daughters while Rosemary watched and little Anne Marie, eight, became pregnant. Luckily, the pregnancy was terminated, as it was ectopic. In later years, both Anne Marie and her sister Heather could not take it any longer and left home.

Fred West would film himself raping his daughters until one day his daughter told her friend about it and she in turn told her mother. Her friend's mother went to the police and on August 6th, 1992, the authorities began their investigation which eventually led to the arrest of both Fred and Rosemary. The children were placed in foster care, but the daughter, Heather, could not be located. Social Workers talked with the children and learned that Heather was supposed to be buried under the patio. Based on this information, a search warrant was granted to excavate the garden in search of Heather. What they found was more than they were looking for. Eleven bodies were discovered in total.

On June 30th, 1994, Rosemary and

Fred West were both formally charged with these murders. Before Fred could be sentenced, he hung himself in his jail cell on January 1st, 1995. Rosemary was tried and convicted of ten murders in October of 1995, and was sentenced to life in prison.

Note: "While in prison, Fred West claimed he killed at least another twenty, including children he killed in a barn."

The next several chapters are cases of male Serial Killers that were captured and sentenced accordingly.

Chapter 25
John Wayne Gacy
Victims (33)

AKA The Killer Clown

John Wayne Gacy was born on March 17th, 1942, in Chicago, Illinois, to John and Marion Gacy. He died May 10th, 1994 by lethal injection, at the age of fifty-two.

Gacy's childhood was an abusive

one. His father was an alcoholic who beat his wife and children on a regular basis and he referred to the younger Gacy as a stupid little sissy and a mama's boy. When Gacy was nine years old he was molested by a family friend. At eleven, he developed a blood clot in his head after being hit in the head by a swing and began to have blackouts. His father believed that his son was faking the blackouts; however, Gacy was eventually treated to dissolve the clot.

At twenty years old, John Gacy left home and headed to Las Vegas, Nevada, where he worked for three months at a mortuary before quitting and returning to Chicago. In Chicago, he enrolled in the Northwestern Business College and got hired by the Nunn-Bush Shoe Company in Springfield, Illinois, as a salesperson. It was there that he met fellow employee, Marlynn Myers. Two years later, in September of 1964, he and Marlynn were wed.

After completing his apprenticeship, Gacy was promoted to manager of his department. He became active in local Springfield organizations, joined the

Jaycees, and rose to vice-president of the Springfield chapter by 1965.

Gacy's father-in-law offered him a position managing three Kentucky Fried Chicken restaurants in Waterloo, Iowa. By this time, Gacy had a family: two children, a son named Michael, and a daughter, Christine. Not long after moving to Iowa, Gacy had his first known homosexual experience with a colleague of the Waterloo Jaycees, which he had joined after moving there. Gacy became involved in pornography, drugs, and prostitution on a regular basis, and in 1967 he molested a teenage male employee at one of his restaurants.

Gacy opened a private club in his basement which catered to his employees. He would often encourage his patrons to drink and then make sexual advances towards them. Gacy once permitted a teen to have sex with his wife in order to blackmail the teen into having oral sex with him. However, his little club came to a grinding halt when in March of 1968, two teens – aged fifteen and sixteen – accused Gacy of sexual assault. Gacy was arrested and ordered by the judge to undergo a psychiatric evaluation at the Psychiatric Hospital of the State University of Iowa. Over a seventeen-day period, two doctors concluded that Gacy was mentally competent to stand trial, but that he had an antisocial personality and would likely repeat his sexual behavior.

On December 3rd, 1968, John Wayne Gacy was convicted of sodomy and sentenced to ten years at the Anamosa State Penitentiary in Iowa. That day, his wife filed for a divorce, petitioning for all the matrimonial property and alimony payments. The Court ruled in her favor, and in September, 1969, the divorce was finalized. Gacy never saw his ex-wife or two children ever again.

Gacy was a model prisoner. While in prison, he completed sixteen high school courses, obtained his diploma, helped to secure an increase in the prisoner's daily pay, and supervised several in-prison projects. He was released on parole with a twelve-month probation period on June 18th, 1970. He promptly left Iowa and moved home to live with his mother in

Chicago the next day.

Gacy, with assistance from his mother, bought a house in Chicago, and it wasn't long before he met Carole Hoff, who he married on July 1st, 1972. By this time, however, Gacy had already begun his killing spree. Just eighteen months out of prison, Gacy murdered his first victim.

Timothy McCoy, a boy fifteen years old, was traveling from Michigan to Omaha on January 2nd, 1972, when Gacy picked him up at Chicago's Greyhound Bus Terminal. Gacy brought the boy back to his house, reassuring the boy that he'd return him to the bus station the next morning. Timothy ended up being stabbed to death and buried in a crawl space which was then covered in cement.

Three years later, one of Gacy's employees, John Butkovitch, seventeen years old, disappeared in July. The day before, John had threatened Gacy as Gacy owed him two weeks back pay. According to Gacy, he lured John to his home and then strangled him to death and buried him under the cement floor in the garage. It is interesting to note that John's parents called the police more than one hundred times over a three year period, urging them to investigate Gacy to no avail.

In March of 1976, Gacy's wife left him. As he suddenly had the house to himself, this gave Gacy the opportunity to kill more often, and he didn't waste any time. Between April and October of 1976, Gacy killed a minimum of eight youths between the ages of fourteen and eighteen, seven of whom he buried in his crawl space, and the other beneath his dining room floor. In December of 1976, Gregory Godzik, another employee of Gacy, also went missing. In the time that he worked for Gacy, Gregory had told his family that Gacy had put him to work digging trenches for a drain in the crawl space beneath his house.

John Szyc, nineteen, was a friend of Gregory Godzik and John Butkovich. On January 20th, 1977, he too disappeared. Gacy lured him to his house with the pretext of selling his car to Gacy. John was killed and buried in the crawl space above the body of his friend, Gregory. Gacy then sold John Szyc's car to another of his employees. On March 15th, he then killed Jon Prestidge, age twenty, a young man who was visiting friends in Chicago.

Between July and December 1977, Gacy killed another seven young men between the ages of sixteen and twenty-one, including the son of a Chicago police sergeant. In August 1977, a clue emerged to the disappearance of John Szyc. The employee to whom Gacy had sold Szyc's car was arrested for stealing gasoline from a station while driving the car. When questioned by police, Gacy told officers that Szyc had sold the car to him before leaving town. The police did not pursue the matter further.

Robert Donnelly, nineteen, was abducted by Gacy at gunpoint from a Chicago bus stop on December 30th, 1977. Gacy brought Robert to his house, tortured him with numerous devices, and raped him. Many times, he dunked Robert's head in a bathtub of water until he passed out. Then Gacy would revive him and repeat all over again. Robert was not killed, thank God, and he later testified at Gacy's trial that he was in so much pain that he asked to be killed, to get it over with. Gacy released him after several hours of torture and assault, and Robert went to the police. On January 6th, 1978, Gacy was questioned about the crime and admitted to having slave sex with Donnelly, but that it was consensual and guess what, the police believed him, and no charges were filed.

A month later, on February 16th, 1978, William Kindred, nineteen, disappeared after telling his fiancée that he was spending an evening at a bar. William was the last victim to be buried in the crawl space as it was getting full. Gacy deposited future victims in the Des Plaines River.

The next month, Gacy lured Jeffrey Rignall, twenty-six, into his car, where he instantly chloroformed him and returned with him to his house. Jeffrey was tortured and repeatedly raped into unconsciousness, then driven to Lincoln Park where he was discarded, unconscious but alive, and managed to stagger to his girlfriend's apartment. Police were again informed of the assault, but did not investigate Gacy because Jeffrey knew few details about his assailant, only remembering later that he'd been taken in a black Oldsmobile.

A few weeks later, in April, Jeffrey and his friends staked out the exit on the Expressway where he knew he had been driven until he saw Gacy's distinctive black Oldsmobile. Rignall and his friends then followed Gacy to his house at 8213 West Summerdale street. Shortly after, Jeffrey went to the police. A warrant was issued, and Gacy was arrested on July 15th, 1978.

While Gacy was awaiting trial for the assault of Jeffrey, on December 11th, 1978 he went into a pharmacy to discuss a remodeling job with the storeowner, Phil Torf. Robert Piest, fifteen, overhearing Gacy telling Torf that his firm hired teenage boys, told his mother that a contractor wanted to talk to him about a job, and left the store to talk with the contractor, never to return. The boy's mom filed a missing persons report and the owner of the store told police that the boy left the store to talk to John Gacy. The police called Gacy the next day and he denied even talking to the boy, promising to come to the station to make a statement confirming what he said. He arrived at the police station the next day covered in mud, claiming that he'd been in a car accident, and totally denied any involvement in the boy's disappearance.

When the police did a background check on Gacy, they discovered he was awaiting trial on battery charges, and that he had served time in Iowa for sodomy. Based on this information, the police believed Gacy was lying and involved with the disappearance of Robert Piest. The police requested a search warrant of Gacy's property, which was granted on December 13th, 1978.

Several suspicious items were revealed during the search: driver's licenses for different people, a high school ring engraved 1975, books on homosexuality and pederasty, handcuffs, a piece of two-by-four with holes drilled in the ends, a syringe, boys' clothing, and a photo receipt from the pharmacy where Robert Piest worked part-time. While police continued with their investigation, they decided to assign two two-man surveillance teams to follow Gacy. Gacy, however, picked up on the surveillance and demanded the police cease their operation. When they did not comply, Gacy filed a three quarter million dollar civil law suit against the Des Plaines Police Department. The hearing was scheduled for December 22nd, 1978.

Meanwhile, the investigation continued, and interesting things started to pop up. Police were informed of Gacy's employee, Gregory Godzik's disappearance, the disappearance of John Butkovich, and that the high school ring found in Gacy's house belonged to another missing person, John Szyc. Another employee revealed that Gacy made him dig trenches in the crawl space of Gacy's house.

On the 21st of December, just one day before Gacy's civil suit against the police, a second warrant was obtained to search his house; in particular, to search the crawl space. Upon digging in the crawl space, police discovered several human bones.

Gacy told police officers that he wanted to "clear the air" after being informed that they had found human remains. While being interrogated, Gacy confessed to the police that since 1972, he had murdered approximately twenty-five to thirty people. He went on to tell the police and the district attorney about how he would abduct his victims, torture them, rape them, and eventually kill them and dispose of their bodies.

Gacy said that he would pour quicklime into the crawl space from time to time to hasten the decomposition of the corpses, and said that he had lost count of the number of victims he'd buried there. He told police that the last five victims were thrown off the I-55 bridge into the Des Plaines river as the crawl space under his house had become full. He confessed to strangling young Robert Piest and disposing of his body in the river. He told them he had buried John Butkovitch under his garage. Police eventually recovered four of the five victims in the river.

Between December 1978 and March 1979, criminal technicians commenced to search and remove bodies from Gacy's property. In total, twenty-nine bodies were unearthed, giving families back their loved ones for proper burial. In several cases, bodies still had the ligatures knotted around their necks. Others had gags deep down in their throats.

Identifying the victims took time. Some were identified through their known connection with Gacy. Others by personal affects found at the property. One victim, Michael Bonnin, seventeen, was identified when his fishing license was found at the scene. Of Gacy's identified victims, the youngest were Samuel Stapleton, fourteen, and Michael Marino, fourteen. The oldest were Russell Nelson, twenty-one, and James Mazzara, twenty-one. Eight of the victims have yet to be identified.

On April 9th, 1979, Robert Piest's body was discovered on the banks of the Des Plaines River. His autopsy revealed that paper-like material had been shoved down his throat while he was alive.

On February 6th, 1980, the trial of John Wayne Gacy started in Chicago before Judge Louis Garippo. Gacy was charged with thirty-three counts of murder. Due to the overwhelming media attention in Chicago, the jurors had to be selected from Rockford, Illinois.

Before going to trial, Gacy's lawyers spent hundreds of hours with doctors at the Menard Correctional Center while psychiatrists conducted tests to determine whether Gacy was mentally fit to stand trial. Gacy, with all his wisdom, tried to convince the doctors that he suffered from multiple personality disorder, but the doctor's decided otherwise. His lawyers opted to plead not guilty by reason of insanity, and did manage to find experts who testified at the trial that they believed Gacy to be a paranoid schizophrenic who indeed suffered from multiple personality disorders. The prosecution's experts, however, stated that Gacy was sane and in full control of his actions. They produced numerous witnesses to testify that his actions were premeditated. Employees testified about digging trenches for Gacy, which they were told was for some kind of drainage system.

The trial went into its fifth week with

the prosecution bringing in dozens of people to testify. The defense only brought in a few people, which infuriated Gacy. On March 11th, 1980, both sides began their final arguments. Terry Sullivan, the prosecutor, presented a summary of Gacy's history of abuse on youths and recapped the testimony given by the surviving witnesses, Donnelly and Voorhees, who had been abused and tortured. After four hours of summation, Robert Motta, for the defense, rebutted the doctor's testimony for the prosecution and tried to portray Gacy as a "man driven by compulsions he was unable to control."

It took the jury less than two hours deliberation to find John Wayne Gacy guilty of all thirty three murders. The defense asked for life without parole, but the prosecution was adamant that he wanted a death sentence for Gacy, which had only came into effect in June of 1977 in the state of Illinois. The jury deliberated again on the fate of Gacy and in only two hours sentenced him to death.

On May 9th, 1994, Gacy was transferred to the Stateville Correctional

Center to be executed. That afternoon he was allowed a picnic on the prison grounds with his family. That evening, a priest prayed with him before going to the chamber.

Prior to beginning of the execution, the chemicals unexpectedly solidified, clogging the I.V. tubing so that the team had to replace the clogged tube and start over. The procedure took eighteen minutes to complete. Before the chemicals started to flow, Gacy was asked if he had any last words. His reply was, "Kiss my ass."

William Kunkle was one of the prosecutors. He summed up the execution pretty good by saying, "He still got a much easier death than any of his victims. In my opinion he got an easier death than he deserved, but the important thing is that he paid for his crimes with his life."

Chapter 26
Ted Bundy
Victims (30+)

Theodore "Ted" Bundy was born on November 24th, 1946 in Burlington, Vermont, to Eleanor Cowell. The identity of his father was never determined. It is suspected that Bundy's father was Eleanor's abusive and violent father, Sam

Cowell.   Bundy was raised by his grandparents in Philadelphia, told that they were his parents and Eleanor was his big sister. Bundy didn't find out the truth about his birth records until 1969 and then resented his mother for lying about his identity.

At nineteen years old, Bundy spent one year at the (UPS) University of Puget Sound. In 1965, he dropped out, and the next year enrolled in Chinese studies at the University of Washington, from which he graduated in 1972. After graduating, Bundy joined Governor Daniel Evan's reelection campaign. Evan's was reelected, and subsequently Bundy was hired as an assistant to the Ross Davis, Chairman of the Washington State Republican Party, who described Bundy as aggressive and smart. In 1973, Bundy was accepted into the law school at UPS to become a lawyer.

On January 4th, 1974, Joni Lenz, eighteen years old, a student at the University of Washington, was alone in her basement apartment when Bundy entered, battered her with a metal rod, and raped her with it, causing her massive internal injuries. Lenz remained unconscious for ten days, and lived through the attack, albeit with permanent brain damage. In February, Bundy struck again, late at night. Lynda Ann Healy, twenty-one, was a student at the University of Washington and a radio weather broadcaster for a Seattle radio station. Bundy broke into her room, beat her unconscious, dressed her, and then carried her away. Her skull was later found on Taylor Mountain. In March, Donna Gail Manson, nineteen, a student at The Evergreen State College, left her dorm on her way to a concert but never made it. To this day, her body had never been found.

Susan Elaine Rancourt, nineteen, disappeared on April 17th, 1974. Susan was abducted from the campus of Central Washington State University in Ellensburg while on her way to meet a friend to see a movie. Her skull too was later found on Taylor Mountain. That night, two other female students suffered attempted abductions, and reported that the man had been wearing his an arm in a sling, and had asked for help to carry books to his

Volkswagen Beetle. It seemed that Bundy was taking one female student per month, which indicated a "cooling off" period according to FBI profilers.

Roberta Kathleen Parks, twenty-three, left her dorm at Oregon State University to have coffee with her friends on May 6th, 1974, and never arrived. Her skull was later found on Taylor Mountain, but not her body. It is interesting to note that, in 1974, Bundy worked at the Washington State Department of Emergency Services, the government agency involved in the search for these missing women.

In the meantime, citizens, students, and parents alike, were concerned about the missing young females, as was the Seattle Police Department, and in particular the Crimes Against Persons Unit. Unfortunately, the police did not have much to go on; there was little to no physical evidence found, and the only common factor between the attacks was that the girls were all white college students, attractive, and wore their hair long and parted in the middle.

On June 1st , 1974, another young girl went missing. Brenda Carol Ball, twenty-two, was last seen leaving the Flame Tavern in Burien talking with a man who had his arm in a sling. Brenda's body was never found, but her skull was found on Taylor Mountain. Just ten days later, on June 11th, another University of Washington student, Georgeann Hawkins, twenty-two, disappeared while walking between her sorority house and her boyfriend's dorm residence. The CSI searched the area with a fine toothed comb and came up with nothing. Once the disappearance of Georgeann was made public, witnesses came forward and reported seeing a man that night on crutches with his leg in a cast. One young woman said that the man asked her to help him carry his briefcase to his brown Volkswagen Beetle. Georgeann's bones were later found with two other bodies near Lake Sammamish Park. Her remains were cremated accidentally by the coroner's office along with those of unidentified persons.

The missing young women and the

brutal attack on Joni Lenz attracted significant exposure from television and newspapers throughout the states of Oregon and Washington. Hitchhiking by women dropped off and the general population lived in fear. The police had no evidence, only a general description of the assailant and his Beetle. Then a month later, on July 14th, and in broad daylight, two women were abducted from a crowded beach at Lake Sammamish State Park in Issaquah. The abduction was witnessed by five females who gave a description to authorities: a young handsome man wearing a white tennis outfit with his left arm in a sling, and who spoke with a slight accent, perhaps Canadian or British. He told the girls that his name was Ted and he'd asked for help to unload a small boat from his Volkswagen Beetle. One girl offered to help him, but when she got close to the car and realized that he did not have a boat, she ran off. Three witnesses reported seeing him approach Janice Anne Ott, twenty-three, a probation caseworker at the court, who left with Bundy. Her body was never discovered. Also on the same day, about four hours later, Denise Naslund, eighteen, was having a picnic and went to the bathroom at the beach. Her body was found two months later.

Because of witnesses providing detailed information about Bundy, the police provided the public with a suspect description and car details and posted fliers all around the Seattle area. A sketch of the abductor was printed in newspapers and broadcast on the TV stations. Several women, including now crime author, Ann Rule, who had once worked with Bundy, recognized the sketch and the car and reported to the police that it was Ted Bundy in the picture. Detectives, however, found it hard to believe that a clean-cut law student with absolutely no criminal record could be the perpetrator.

On September 6th, 1974, hunters stumbled across skeletal remains in the woods in Issaquah. The bones were later identified as those of Janice Ott and Georgeann Hawkins. Six months later, several skulls were found on Taylor Mountain; all were damaged from a blunt instrument.

Bundy received an acceptance letter from the University of Utah Law School in August, 1974, and moved to Salt Lake City. As his picture was being plastered everywhere, it is assumed that he moved to avoid being caught, even though he was not a suspect at the time.

After Bundy moved to Utah, young women started to disappear. On September 2nd, he strangled and raped a hitchhiker in Idaho who, to this day, has yet to be identified, and the next day returned to where he dumped her to dismember and photograph her corpse. Exactly one month later on October 2nd, Nancy Wilcox, sixteen, was taken and brought into a wooded area where Bundy raped and killed her by strangulation. Her body was never found.

Melissa Smith, seventeen, was the daughter of the Chief of Police in Midvale, Utah. Melissa left a pizza parlor where she had been visiting with her friends, but never arrived home. Her body was found on October 27th in Summit Park, nine days after she'd been abducted. The autopsy indicated that she might have remained alive for up to seven days before she was killed. On October 31st, Laura Aime, seventeen, also disappeared after leaving a café. Her body was found by hikers in American Fork Canyon. She had been sodomized, raped, beaten, and strangled.

Carol DaRonch, eighteen, is alive and well, and one brave young woman. She is today the only living victim of Ted Bundy. Carol was at a mall window-shopping in November when a man presented himself as Office Roseland of the Murray Police Department and told Carol that someone had tried to break into her car. He asked if she would come with him to the station to file a complaint. When Carol pointed out that Bundy was driving on a road that did not lead to the police station, he immediately pulled to the shoulder and attempted to handcuff her. Carol got a lucky break. During their struggle Bundy unintentionally fastened both handcuffs to the same wrist, and DaRonch was able to open the car door and escape, but not before Bundy threatened her with a gun. Swinging a crowbar, DaRonch screamed, scratched, and squirmed, until finally she burst out of the car. Carol immediately went to the police and gave her account of an attempted kidnapping, which subsequently gained disturbing weight when Debra Kent's disappearance was reported later that evening. The next morning, investigators found a handcuff key in the high school parking lot. Later that same evening, Debra Kent, seventeen, a student at Viewmont High School in Bountiful, disappeared after leaving a theater production at the school to pick up her brother. The school's drama teacher, and a student, told police that a stranger had asked each of them to come out to the parking lot to identify a car. Another student later saw the same man pacing in the rear of the auditorium, and the drama teacher spotted him again shortly before the end of the play. Debra's body has never been found to this day.

From his home base in Utah, in 1975, Bundy switched his hunting ground to Colorado, and on January 12th, Caryn Campbell, twenty-three, a registered nurse, disappeared while walking down the hall of the Wildwood Inn in Snowmass. Her nude body was discovered next to a dirt road a month later. Autopsy reports showed deep cuts from a sharp instrument and blunt force trauma to the head.

The killing continued. Julie Cunningham, twenty-six, Denise Oliverson, twenty-five, and Lynette Culver, twelve, were all killed between March and May of 1975.

The King County Police compiled all pertinent information they had to try to come up with a suspect. Their eventual list of twenty-six suspects included known sex offenders, Volkswagen owners, classmates, and acquaintances of each victim. In the end, Bundy's name was at the top when word came about his arrest in Utah.

A Utah Highway Patrolman in Granger, Salt Lake City, arrested Bundy in August of 1975 after he failed to stop for a routine check. The Patrolman noticed that the front passenger seat in the car was missing, and while searching the car discovered a ski mask, a crowbar, handcuffs, a coil of rope, trash bags, an ice pick, and other items that one would use in the process of committing a burglary. Bundy tried to explain that he'd found many of the items; however, Detective Jerry Thompson remembered the suspect and car description in the attempted abduction of Carol DaRonch, and the phone calls from Kloepher back in December of 1974. In a search of Bundy's apartment, police found a guide to Colorado ski resorts with a checkmark by the Wildwood Inn, and a brochure advertising the Viewmont High School play in Bountiful where Debra Kent had disappeared, but they had nothing adequately incriminating to hold him. He was released under his own cognizance and, without his knowing, placed on 24-hour surveillance.

In February, 1975, Bundy had to stand trial for the kidnapping of DaRonch. Judge Stewart Hanson found him guilty of kidnapping and assault on March 1st and sentenced Bundy to 1-15 years in prison. Also, he was charged with the Colorado murder of Caryn Campbell and was extradited to Aspen in January of 1977.

After electing to serve as his own attorney, Bundy was excused by the judge from wearing handcuffs and leg irons. On June 7th, 1977, Bundy asked permission to use the law library at the courthouse to research his case. From behind a bookcase, he opened a window and jumped from the second floor. He then hiked to the southern part of Aspen Mountain while roadblocks were being set up by police.

Bundy broke into a hunting cabin near the mountain summit and stole clothes, food, and a rifle. The next day he continued south but got lost in the woods. Over the next few days, he continued moving around, breaking into camp trailers to steal food, and managed to avoid search parties and roadblocks. Three days later, Bundy managed to steal a car but police caught him weaving in and out of a lane and he was recaptured.

Bundy was sent back to jail in Glenwood Springs where he wasted no time in planning another escape despite the advice of friends and legal advisors to stay put. Over a period of six months, Bundy acquired a hacksaw blade from another prisoner and built up about $500 in cash which was smuggled in to him by visitors; in particular, Carole Ann Boone. During the evenings while other inmates were showering, Bundy sawed a hole approximately one foot square in the corner ceiling of his cell, and after losing thirty-five pounds, was able to move through the crawl space during his practice tries.

On the night of December 30th, while most of the jail staff was on Christmas break, and many of the short-term prisoners were released to spend the holidays with their families, Bundy stacked books on his bed under a blanket to make it look like he was sleeping, and slipped into the crawl space. He broke through the ceiling into the apartment of the chief guard who happened to be out for the evening with his wife, changed into street clothes from the guard's closet, and walked out the front door to freedom. The escape was not detected until the next day. By then Bundy had a seventeen-hour head start. He stole a car and drove out of Glenwood Springs; the car broke down and

SERIAL KILLERS CASE FILES

he hitched a ride into Vail, caught a bus to Denver, and a flight to Chicago. He was in Chicago by the time the guards noticed he was missing. From there he bussed to Ann Arbor, Michigan, and five days later stole a car and drove to Atlanta where he caught another bus to Tallahassee, Florida. He rented a room under the alias Chris Hagen at a boarding house near Florida State University.

On January 15th, 1978, Bundy entered a sorority house on campus and killed Margaret Bowman, twenty-one, with a piece of firewood while she was asleep, and proceeded to garrote her with a nylon stocking. In the same room, he attacked Lisa Levy, twenty, beat her unconscious, sexually assaulted her with a bottle, literally tore off one of her nipples, and then strangled her. In the next bedroom, he attacked Kathy Kleiner, who suffered a broken jaw and deep shoulder lacerations, and Karen Chandler, who suffered a concussion, broken jaw, loss of teeth, and a crushed finger. Both Chandler and Kleiner survived however, only to suffer a lifetime of physical and emotional stress. The police were called immediately.

On February 15th, 1978, Officer David Lee was on car patrol when he noticed a yellow Volkswagen Bug idling in an alley behind a restaurant. It was late and the restaurant was closed so it was suspicious that someone was there in a car. Officer Lee went past but watched the car in his rearview mirror as the car pulled out of the alley and headed in the opposite direction. Officer Lee turned around to follow the car, and as he drove he radioed in the car's license plate number. The plates came back as stolen, and Officer Lee started pursuit of the car, which sped up and began a series of elusive maneuvers. Finally, the car stopped, at which time Officer Lee drew his gun and approached the car with caution.

Bundy was ordered out of the car and advised that he was under arrest. Bundy kicked Officer Lee's legs out from underneath him and took off at a run. Officer Lee gave chase and tackled Bundy to the ground. Both struggled over the gun but Officer Lee won, subdued Bundy, and placed him under arrest. As Officer Lee was transporting his prisoner to the lockup, he was not aware that he just arrested one of the F.B.I.'s Ten Most Wanted Fugitives, but he did hear Bundy say, "I wish you had killed me."

Ted Bundy's trial was televised and quickly became a media circus. Bundy did not want a lawyer and once again represented himself. He did a poor job, according to many lawyers, and in July of 1979 was found guilty and sentenced to death. On the evening before his execution, Bundy reviewed his confessed victim tally on a state-by-state basis with officials. He killed;

11 in Washington - 3 unidentified

8 in Utah - 3 unidentified

3 in Colorado

3 in Florida

2 in Oregon - both unidentified

2 in Idaho - 1 unidentified

1 in California - unidentified

Ted Bundy died in the Raiford electric chair at 7:16 am on January 24th, 1989. He managed to live 10 years in prison.

Chapter 27
Donald Henry Gaskins
Victims (40 to 181)

Donald Henry Gaskins was born on March 13th, 1933, in Florence County, South Carolina. Gaskins spent a great deal of his childhood in reform schools, and because of his short stature, just 5' 4", was dubbed Pee Wee, a name which contributed to him being subjected to physical abuse, and later, in prison, sexual abuse. Gaskins did not do well in school and elected to be a petty criminal. He married in 1951 at the age of eighteen, and the following year had a daughter. His marriage did not last long as he attacked a teenage girl and hit her with a hammer. He was arrested and sentenced to six years at the Central Correctional Institution. During his imprisonment, his wife divorced him.

While he was in prison, Gaskin's committed his first murder. He slashed the throat of another inmate, Hazel Brazell. His reasoning for killing Brazell was to earn a reputation so that the other prisoners would fear him. He only got an additional three years added on to his sentence however as he claimed it was in self-defense. Just two years later, in 1955, he escaped prison by hiding out in the back of a garbage truck and fled to Florida. He was arrested again but eventually paroled in 1961.

After his release, Gaskins went back to his petty crimes, stealing and breaking into businesses. He was arrested again in 1963 for the rape of a twelve-year-old girl and sentenced to eight years in the pen. He was released in 1968 after serving only five of those years and swore that he would never go back to prison again. Gaskins then moved to the town of Sumter where he worked as a laborer with a construction company. In September of 1969, Gaskins began his killing spree.

In September 1969, The Redneck picked up a female hitchhiker and started flirting with her. When she laughed at him, he pounded her unconscious, raped, sodomized, and tortured her; he then threw her into a swamp, still alive. This was the first of his so-called 'Coastal Kills.' He later referred to the Coastal Kills as the random killing of people in which, prior to killing, he sometimes enjoyed torturing his victims for days. He would at times cannibalize their dismembered bodies while they watched and force them to eat their own flesh.

He was not what the FBI would refer to as an organized killer. He had no preference; he would kill children, women, and men, but in November of 1970, Gaskins commenced what he would call his 'Serious Murders' of people he knew, such as family and friends. His niece, Janice Kirby, fifteen, and her friend, Patricia

Alsobrook, seventeen, were the first victims of his Serious Murders. He took the girls to an abandoned house where he beat and raped them before drowning them.

Gaskins later bought an old hearse while living in Prospect, South Carolina. When asked why he bought a hearse he once said, "I kill so many people I need a vehicle to haul all the bodies to my private cemetery," but of course the person he said it to did not take him seriously. He did have friends, and one was Doreen Dempsey, twenty-three, a pregnant single mom of a two year old. She asked Gaskins for a ride to the bus station as she was moving to another town. Gaskins took her to a wooded area instead where he started fondling the little two year old girl. When Doreen tried to stop him he smashed her skull, raped and sodomized the girl, and then raped and killed Doreen. He later said to authorities that it was the best sex he'd had in his life.

Suzanne Kipper paid Gaskins $1500 to kill Silas Yates, a wealthy farmer in Florence County, and he agreed. One night, Gaskins and a few of his ex-con friends,

John Power, John Owens, and Diane Neely, planned and killed Yates, after which they buried his body. Shortly afterward, Diane Neely and her boyfriend, Avery Howard, attempted to blackmail Gaskins for $5000, or they would inform about the Yates' murder. Gaskins killed both Howard and Neely and dumped their bodies. Gaskins had another friend by the name of Walter Neely who helped Gaskins kill and dispose of two men who had attempted to steal from him. Gaskins showed Neely where he disposed of all the bodies he had killed, which he said totaled 181 people. Walter Neely eventually could not stand knowing that all those people were killed and went to the police.

After authorities obtained search warrants, they discovered nine bodies of several of Gaskins' family and friends. He was tried, convicted, and sentenced to death, but in November of 1976 his sentence was changed to life in prison when the South Carolina General Assembly death sentence rule of 1974 was altered to conform to the United States Supreme Court's guidelines for the death penalty.

After being in prison for six years, Gaskins committed another murder that earned him the title of 'Meanest Man in America.' An inmate named Rudolph Tyner had once killed an elderly couple named Myrtle and Bill Moon during a robbery of their store that the Moon's owned. Gaskin was hired as a hitman by Tony Cimo, the son of Myrtle Moon, to kill Tyner, which he did on September 2nd, 1982. Rather craftily, Gaskins' rigged a device similar to a small radio in Tyner's cell and told him that they would be able to communicate back and forth, but when Tyner held the speaker to his ear as Gaskins instructed him to do, the small device exploded as it contained a charge of C4. Gaskins later said that, "The last thing Tyner heard was me laughing." By this time, the death penalty was reinstated in the state of South Carolina.

While Gaskins was on death row he confessed to 181 murders. Whether he can be believed or not, we may never know. At 1:10am on September 6th, 1991, Gaskins was electrocuted. His last words were, "I'll let my lawyers talk for me. I'm ready to go."

Chapter 28
Gary Ridgway
Victims (49)

The Green River Killer

Gary Leon Ridgway was born on February 18th, 1949 in Salt Lake City, Utah, to Mary and Thomas Ridgway. He has two brothers, Thomas Jr., and Gregory.

As a youngster, Ridgway witnessed several violent disagreements between his overbearing mother and his father. Ridgway was a bed wetter, which is common in serial killers, and his mother would often humiliate and demean him in front of friends and family because of it. He had mixed feelings of sexual attraction towards his mother as well as annoyance. He was also not very bright as a child, testing at an IQ of only 82. He performed below academic standards for his age and had to repeat at least one grade twice.

When Ridgway was sixteen years old he led another boy into the woods where he stabbed him in the back and punctured his liver. Ridgway laughed as he left, and said, "I always wondered what it would be like to kill someone." Luckily, the boy survived.

Ridgway joined the U.S. Navy at twenty, shortly after marrying his high school sweetheart, Claudia Barrows, who was nineteen at the time. He was sent overseas to Vietnam where he spent a great deal of time with prostitutes and contracted gonorrhea. Although it irritated him, he did not bother using condoms and continued to have unprotected sex with them. Meanwhile, back home, his wife was also unfaithful and within a year their marriage ended.

After returning home from Nam, Ridgway met and married Marcia Winslow, but he could not prevent himself from being unfaithful to her either. He continued to frequent prostitutes even though, while doing so, he professed to be religious. He would go to church on Sunday, and preached the bible door to door; he would often cry after sermons, and annoy people at his work regarding the bible. While portraying this self-righteous religious persona, he would participate in sexual deviations with prostitutes and always wanted Marsha to have sex with him in public places. Regardless of all of this, his wife gave him a son, Matthew, in 1975.

It is believed that from 1982 to 1998, Ridgway took the lives of seventy-one women, but that number could be much higher. He was dubbed 'The Green River Killer' in the early 1980s when his first five victims were found in the Green River near Seattle in the state of Washington.

Most of Ridgway's murders were prostitutes he'd picked up. He'd show them a picture of his son, take them to a secluded area or just to his truck, have sex with and then strangle them. Initially, he would strangle them using his hands, but found that when they fought back they would scratch or mark him, so he began to use a ligature instead.

A task force was set up by the King County Sheriff's Office named the Green River Task Force. As this was obviously the work of a serial rapist/killer, and hence a Federal crime, the Federal Bureau of Investigation soon became involved. The mid 1980s was also the start of what the F.B.I. calls 'profiling.' In short, profiling is a behavioral and investigative means that is intended to assist investigators to profile unidentified criminal subjects or offenders. Offender profiling is also known as criminal profiling, criminal personality profiling, criminological profiling, behavioral profiling, or criminal investigative analysis.

The Green River Killer later stated, when he was incarcerated, that he had killed so many women that he'd lost count. Most of his victims he would either dump in the Green River or in a wooded area that he would visit frequently. Ridgway would often return to his victims to have sex with the corpses (an act of necrophilia). He would also bring debris such as cigarette butts, and gum to contaminate the area, in case the police found the bodies. That way, they wouldn't find just his D.N.A. alone.

Ridgway was arrested on a prostitution charge in 1982 and by 1983 he was a suspect in the Green River killings. He was given a polygraph test, however, and passed it. Unfortunately, it wasn't until 1987 that police obtained a DNA test from Ridgway. In 1982, Ridgway killed sixteen women and twenty-three in 1983. He killed another ten after that, spread out over several years. Again, this are confirmed kills. Most likely the actual numbers were higher.

Judith Mawson married Ridgway in 1988 after dating for three years. Around this time, Ridgway stopped killing. He later said that once he was in a relationship with Mawson, the urge to kill was not there for him because he truly loved her.

As I said a couple paragraphs back, his DNA was collected in 1987 for analysis. Back then it took a long time to acquire comparison results. On November 30th,

2001, the police arrived at Ridgway's place of work, the Kenworth Truck Factory, with an arrest warrant in hand.

Ridgway, the serial killer, was arrested for the murder of four women; Opal Mills, sixteen, killed on August 12th, 1982; Marcia Chapman, thirty-one, killed on August 1st, 1982; Cynthia Hinds, seventeen, killed on August 11th, 1982; and Carol Ann Christensen, twenty-one, killed May 3rd, 1983. Obviously the F.B.I. have not connected Ridgway to all the killings yet because Carol Ann was actually his twenty-third killing. After the indictment, and more evidence was obtained, three more victims were added to the charges of murder: Wendy Coffield, sixteen, killed July 8th, 1982 (Wendy was Ridgway's first victim); Debra Bonner, twenty-three, killed July 25th, 1982; and Debra Estes, fifteen, killed September 20th, 1982.

The Green River Killer was finally captured, and on December 18th, 2001, Ridgway was arraigned on charges of multiple murders and brought into the courtroom by several security officers. He seemed relaxed during his ten-minute appearance. Aloud, prosecutor Jeff Baird read the detailed charges for each victim, mentioning their names each time, saying that Ridgway caused the death of each woman, and referred to them all as human beings. In reply, Ridgway's defense attorney, Tony Savage, said, "His plea is not guilty to all charges. Let them prove it. I don't think they can." Ridgway was ordered to appear in court again on January 2nd, 2002, when the King County prosecutors would be seeking the death penalty. In the meantime, Ridgway was held without bail.

It was reported in August of 2003 that his lawyers, led by Anthony Savage, were close to a plea bargain deal that would spare Ridgway the death penalty in return for his confession and assistance in locating the victims in the Green River murders. So, on November 5th, 2003, Ridgway entered a guilty plea to forty-eight charges of motivated murder in the first degree as part of the plea bargain that would spare him execution. In exchange, he would collaborate in locating the remains of his victims and provide other details. In his statement supplementing his guilty plea, Ridgway explained that all of his victims had been killed inside King County, Washington, and that he had transported and deposited the remains of the two other women near Portland just to confuse the police.

On December 18th, 2003, King County Superior Court Judge, Richard Jones, sentenced Ridgway to forty-eight life sentences with no possibility of parole, and one life sentence, to be served consecutively. He was also sentenced to an additional ten years for tampering with evidence for each of the forty-eight victims, adding 480 years to his forty-eight life sentences.

Ridgway resides at the Washington State Penitentiary in Walla Walla, Washington where another notorious killer lives, Kenneth Bianchi, the Hillside Strangler.

Chapter 29
Jeffrey Dahmer
Victims (17)

The Milwaukee Monster

Jeffrey Lionel Dahmer was born on May 21st, 1960, in West Allis, Wisconsin, to Lionel and Joyce (nee Flint) Dahmer. Jeffrey was considered a normal boy until around ten years old. However, he lacked interest in activities or hobbies; he withdrew from friends and family; he would ride around on his bike in search of dead animals so that he could take them home and dissect them. He once went to the extreme of putting a stake in a dog's head. By the time he reached his teens, Dahmer was a full-blown alcoholic.

At seventeen years old, Dahmer was always having fantasies about killing men and having sex with their dead bodies, but he did not act on his fantasy until just after he graduated high school in June, 1978. He picked up a hitchhiker, Steven Hicks, nineteen. They had sex, drank beer, and after that, Hicks wanted to go home. Dahmer did not want Hicks to leave and struck him in the head with a ten-pound barbell, killing him. Needing to dispose of the body, Dahmer cut the body up, packaged it in plastic garbage bags, and buried the bags in the woods behind his home. That was his first kill. It would be another nine years before he killed again.

Dahmer went on to attend the University of Ohio State for one semester. He drank most of the time, missed a lot of classes, dropped out, and then signed up for the U.S. Army. Of course, being an alcoholic, his stint in the army did not last long. Two years later, in 1981, he was discharged and went to live with his grandmother in West Allis where he lived for the next six years.

On September 15th, 1987, Dahmer was in a hotel room with Steven Toumi, twenty-six, after spending the night at a popular gay bar. Dahmer later confessed that he did not know how he killed Toumi, but when he woke up, Steven was dead, and he had blood on his mouth. He went to a store, bought a large suitcase, stuffed the body inside it, took the suitcase to his grandmother's basement, had sex with the corpse, masturbated on it, dismembered it, and threw it in the garbage.

While staying at his grandmother's, she noticed increasingly strange behaviors in her grandson over time. She found a fully dressed male mannequin in his bedroom closet; another time she found a .357 Magnum pistol under his bed, and then there was that terrible smell coming from the basement which Dahmer said was just a dead squirrel he'd brought home and dissolved with chemicals. In 1982 he was arrested twice for indecent exposure and then, in 1986, masturbated in front of two boys and was arrested again, but only got a slap on the wrist.

His grandmother had had enough of his weird behavior, the foul smells in the basement, the arrests, his late night outs. In 1988 she asked him to leave. At the time Dahmer was working at a Chocolate Factory and decided to get an apartment closer to his work on the west side of Milwaukee. Just one day after he moved into his apartment on September 27th, 1988, he was arrested again for drugging and sexually molesting a thirteen-year-old boy. He was found guilty, fired from his job, sentenced to five years probation and one year working in a release camp for offenders, and was required by law to register as a sex offender.

Dahmer worked the release camp, was paroled two months early, and moved into a new apartment. Soon after moving in, he began his murder binge.

In 1988 and 1989, Dahmer killed James   Doxtator,   fourteen;   Richard

Guerrero, twenty-five; and Anthony Sears, twenty-six. He would party with them, have sex, murder them, dismember them, masturbate on their corpses, and then store them in the basement. Keeping the skull of Anthony Sears, he boiled it to remove the skin, painted it gray to make it look like a plastic model, and saved the trophy for two years – until it was recovered from his apartment on July 23rd, 1991. Later he explained that he used to masturbate in front of the skull for gratification.

In May of 1990, Dahmer moved into the apartment that later would become infamous: Apartment 213, 924 North 25th Street, Milwaukee.

In 1990, Dahmer picked the pace up of his killings. He murdered Eddie Smith, thirty-six, in June; Ricky Beeks, twenty-seven, in July; Ernest Miller, twenty-two, in September; David Thomas, twenty-three, also in September; Curtis Straughter, nineteen, in February 1991; Errol Lindsey, nineteen, in April; and Tony Hughes, thirty-one, in May.

In the wee hours of May 27th, 1991,

Konerak Sinthasomphone, fourteen, was discovered wandering naked on the street, heavily drugged and bleeding from his rectum. Two young women from the neighborhood found the confused young boy and called 911. Dahmer chased after the boy to take him back to his apartment, but the women stopped him. When the police arrived, Dahmer told them that Sinthasomphone was his nineteen-year-old boyfriend, and they'd had an argument while drinking. The two women were not pleased and protested, but the two police officer turned the boy over to Dahmer. The police later reported a strange smell inside Dahmer's apartment, but did not investigate it. The smell was the body of Tony Hughes, Dahmer's previous victim, decomposing in the bedroom. The two policemen did not try to verify the boy's age and also failed to run the background check that would have revealed Dahmer as a convicted child molester, registered sex offender, and still on probation. Later that night, Dahmer killed and dismembered the young lad, keeping his skull as a souvenir. *Author Note: Officers Joseph P. Gabrish and John A. Balcerzak were fired after this incident but appealed and were re-instated.*

On June 30th, 1991, Dahmer killed Matt Turner, twenty; Jeremiah Weinberger, twenty-three, on July 5th; Oliver Lacy, twenty-three, on July 12th; and Joseph Brandehoft, twenty-five, on July 19th. While the victims were still alive, Dahmer would drill holes into their skulls and inject hydrochloric acid into their frontal lobes with a syringe to make them into submissive zombies, and then have sex with them. Residents of the Oxford Apartment building noticed terrible odors coming from Apartment 213, as well as the thumps of falling objects and the occasional buzzing of a power saw.

A young man by the name of Tracy Edwards is Dahmer's only known living survivor and in my eyes, a hero.

On July 22nd, 1991, Dahmer enticed Tracy Edwards into his home. According to Tracy's later testimony, Dahmer struggled with Edwards in order to handcuff him, but failed to cuff his wrists together. With a large knife in his hand, Dahmer forced

Edwards into the bedroom where Edwards saw pictures of mangled bodies on the wall and noticed the terrible stench coming from a large blue barrel. Edwards turned and punched Dahmer in the face, kicked him in the stomach, ran out the door, and escaped. As he ran through the streets, he still had the handcuffs hanging from one hand, but Edwards waved for help at a police car driven by Officer Robert Rauth and Officer Rolf Mueller of the Milwaukee police department.

Edwards took the Officers back to Dahmer's apartment where Dahmer acted friendly towards them. However, remembering that the knife Dahmer had threatened him with was in the bedroom, Edwards asked the police to check.

When one of the officers checked the bedroom, he saw the photographs of mangled bodies, and called for his partner to arrest Dahmer. As one Officer restrained Dahmer, the other opened the refrigerator and found a human head. A search of the apartment revealed three more decapitated heads, multiple photographs of murdered victims and human remains, severed hands and penises, and pictures of dismembered victims and human remains in his refrigerator. The officers called for backup and C.S.I. agents. Dahmer was taken into custody. Once the media was alerted, the notorious apartment gained infamy. It was reported that several bodies were stored in acid filled vats, he kept human skulls in his closet, and a human heart in the freezer. It was soon believed that Jeffrey Dahmer was not only a serial rapist/killer, but also a cannibal and necrophiliac.

Dahmer was indicted on seventeen murders; however, he was not charged with the attempted murder of Tracy Edwards. On January 30th, 1992, his trial began with overwhelming evidence consisting of not only pictures but also body parts. He was found guilty and sentenced to 957 years in prison.

Dahmer was incarcerated at the Columbia Correctional Institution. During his short stay, he professed to be a "born again Christian."

In prison, Dahmer was attacked twice. In July of 1994, another inmate tried to slit his throat with a razor while Dahmer was returning from the prison chapel. Dahmer was only wounded. He was not so lucky on November 28th, 1994 when a prisoner by the name of Christopher Scarver beat Dahmer over the head in the prison gym with a broomstick. Dahmer died on the way to the hospital. When asked why he'd attacked Dahmer, Scarver replied, "It was the work of God."

Chapter 30
Dennis Rader
Victims (10)

The BTK Killer

Dennis Rader was born on March 9th, 1945 in Wichita, Kansas, to William and Dorothea Rader, the oldest of four boys. As a young boy in grade school, according to his own admission, he fantasized about tying up girls and having his way with them. He tortured small animals and had a fetish for women's panties.

At twenty-one years old, Rader joined the U.S. Air Force where he spent four years in active duty stationed in various places around the world. He had an honorable discharge in 1970 as Sergeant and received medals for marksmanship, good conduct, and defense service. By all indications, he was a good, upstanding soldier. Later in life, when he was arrested, his comrades were very shocked.

Once he returned stateside, Rader continued to lead a normal life. He got a job at a local IGA supermarket, remained in the reserves, went to the Community College, and got a degree in Electronics in 1973. He later attended Wichita State University and in 1979 graduated with a degree in Administration of Justice. On May 22nd, 1971, he married Paula Dietz and had two children. Everything appeared normal on the outside, but in his mind Rader still maintained his fantasies of binding, torturing, and killing women. He would walk or drive around and admire women until in 1974, he decided to act on his desires and calculated a plan.

A new Hispanic family had recently moved into Rader's neighborhood. One day, while dropping his wife off where she worked at the hospital, he noticed this beautiful Hispanic woman with dark hair, which he liked. He scouted the house for several days trying to get a routine of the family's activities, and concluded that he could strike in the morning after the husband went to work. On January 15th, 1974, at 8 a.m., Rader crept around the house and cut the telephone wire. But as Murphy's Law would have it, the entire family was home when Rader broke in: the husband, wife, kids, and the dog. He used his gun and told them he only wanted money and a car to escape as he was a wanted man, and he ordered everyone into the bedroom. Joe Otero, thirty-eight, was killed first as he fought Rader to keep from putting a bag over his head. Rader then proceeded to strangle and kill Joe Jr., aged nine, and his sister Josephine, eleven, before he took Julie, thirty-four, to the basement where he hung her and masturbated over her. Rader did not know that the Oteros had three other children who had already gone to school. Those children arrived home to found their family killed.

He killed again 1974, and then "cooled off" until 1977. On April 4th, 1974, he broke into the home of Kathryn Bright, twenty-one, and hid in her bedroom closet until she came home. Again, he was not expecting anyone but Kathryn, but her brother Kevin, nineteen, was out running errands with her and came back to her house. When they entered, Rader came out of the bedroom with his gun and told them that he was a wanted fugitive traveling from California to New York and only needed a car and some money. He instructed Kevin to tie up his sister. Kevin then turned on Rader and put up a fight for their lives, only to be shot in the face. Kevin continued to fight, however, and only stopped when Rader shot him in the head.

Rader thought Kevin was dead and went to work on Kathryn, who also put up a struggle, until Rader stabbed her multiple times. But he then had to make a quick exit when Kevin came to and ran for help. Kathryn died later in the hospital. Kevin Bright is the only known survivor of the BTK killer.

In October of 1974, the killer wrote

to the Wichita Eagle Newspaper describing the murders of the Otero family with details that only the killer could know. He ended the note by saying, "I did it myself with noone's help, the code words for me will be... Bind them, toture them, kill them, B.T.K...." Very poor penmanship and grammar as you can see.

On March 17th, 1977, Shirley Vian, twenty-four, was at home with her children when Rader entered and told her to put the three kids in the bathroom. He told her that he was not going to have his way with her and began binding her. Rader tied her with rope and then strangled her to death. On her panties, lying next to her body, was his semen. He had intended to kill the children as they had seen him, but the phone rang and startled him so he ran off.

Also in 1977, Rader stalked another young woman, and on December 8th, Nancy Fox, twenty-five years old, died at the hands of the BTK killer. As he'd done earlier in the year, he broke into her home and hid out in the bedroom, waiting her arrival; he knew she lived alone. Once she came home, he displayed the same MO.

He used his gun to lure her into the bedroom, tied her to the bed, and strangled her. He later said that before doing so, he told her that he was the killer the police were after. He left more DNA by way of semen on her nightgown.

The next day he went to a random telephone booth and called the police dispatcher. All calls to dispatch are recorded, and this call would later be played numerous times through the media in hopes of someone identifying his voice. He said, "Yes, you will find a homicide at 843 South Pershing. Nancy Fox...That is correct". The police dispatched a unit to the home of Nancy Fox and found her body. No one seemed to recognize the voice, not even his family, wife, or co-workers. Shortly after that, he wrote another letter to the newspaper taking credit for the murders of Shirley Vian, Nancy Fox, the Otero family, and Kathryn Bright. The letter is not edited and is as follows, as he wrote it:

"I find the newspaper not wirting about the poem on Vain unamusing. A little paragraph would have enough. Iknow it not the media fault. The Police Cheif he keep things quiet, and doesn't let the public know there a psycho running around lose strangling mostly women, there 7 in the ground; who will be next? How many do I have to Kill before I get a name in the paper or some national attention. Do the cop think that all those deaths are not related? Golly -gee, yes the M.O. is different in each, but look a pattern is developing. The victims are tie up-most have been women-phone cut- bring some bondage mater sadist tendencies-no struggle, outside the death spot-no wintness except the Vain's Kids. They were very lucky; a phone call save them. I was go-ng to tape the boys and put plastics bag over there head like I did Joseph, and Shirley. And then hang the girl. God-oh God what a beautiful sexual relief that would been.

Josephine, when I hung her really turn me on; her pleading for mercy then the rope took whole, she helpless; staring at me with wide terror fill eyes the rope getting tighter-tighter. You don't understand these things because your not under the influence of factor x). The same thing that made Son of Sam, Jack the Ripper, Havery Glatman, Boston Strangler, Dr. H.H. Holmes Panty Hose Strangler OF Florida, Hillside Strangler, Ted of the West Coast and many more infamous character kill. Which seem s senseless, but we cannot help it. There is no help, no cure, except death or being caught and put away. It a terrible nightmarebut, you see I don't lose any sleep over it. After a thing like Fox I ccome home and go about life like anyone else. And I will be like that until the urge hit me again. It not continuous and I don;t have a lot of time. It take time to set a kill, one mistake and it all over. Since I about blew it on the phone-handwriting is out-letter guide is to long and typewriter can be traced too,.My short poem of death and maybe a drawing;later on real picture and maybe a tape of the sound will come your way. How will you know me. Before a murder or murders you will receive a copy of the initials B.T.K. , you keep that copy the original will show up some day on guess who? "May you not be the unluck one!

P.S.

How about some name for me, its time: 7 down and many more to go. I like the following How about you?

"'THE B.T.K. STRANGLER', WICHITA STRANGLER', 'POETIC STRANGLER', 'THE BOND AGE STRANGLER' OR PSYCHO' THE WICHITA HANGMAN THE WICHITA EXECUTIONER, 'THE GAROTE PHATHOM', 'THE ASPHIXIATER'.

B.T.K."

On a separate piece of paper he wrote:
"#5 You guess motive and victim.

"#6 You found one Shirley Vain lying belly down on a unmade bed in northeast bedroom-hand tied behind back with black tape and cord. Feet & ankles with black tape &legs. Ankles tied to west head of the bed with small off white cord, wrap around legs, hands, arm, finally the neck, many times. A off white pla stic bag over her head loop on with a pink nitie was barefooted. She was sick use a glass of water and smoke I or Two cigarette-house a total mess- kids took some toys with them to the bathroom-bedagainst east

192

bathroom door. Chose at random with some pre-planning. Motive Factor X.

"#7 One Nancy Fox-lying belly down on made bed in southwest bedroom-hands tied behind back with red panty hose-feet together with yellow nitie-semi-nude with pink sweather and bra small neckless-glasses on west dresser-panties below butt-many different than the hosery. She had a smoke and wbnt to the bathroom before the final act-very neat housekeeper& dresser-rifled pursein kitchen-empty paper bag - white coat in living-room- heat up to about 90 degrees, Christsmas tree lights on- nities and hose around the room- hose bag of orange color it and hosery on bed-driver licence gone-seminal stain on or in blue women wear. Chose at random with little pre-planning, Motive Factor "X."

"#8 Next victim maybe: You will find her hanging with a wire noose-Hands behind back with black tape or cord -feet with tape or cord-gaged- then cord around the body to the neck -hooded maybe- possible seminal stain in anus-or on body. Will be chosen at random. Some pre-planning-

Motive Factor 'X'."

Upon receiving this letter in early 1978, the Wichita Police Department made it public that there was an UNSUB, an unknown serial killer on the loose in Wichita. This prompted citizens to be extra vigilant, to check their phone lines as soon as they entered their homes, and to lock doors and windows.

For whatever reason, as who really understands a psychopath, the BTK Killer stopped killing and lived as a regular family man. He had a nine year old son, he was a boy scout leader, and a real upstanding citizen. It is well known after many years of studying serial killers that, according to the FBI, they often go through a "cooling off' period. Seven years passed where Rader killed no one. On April 27th, 1985, he cut the telephone line of one Marine Hedge, fifty-three, and hid in her bedroom waiting for her to come home. Marine came home accompanied by a male friend who stayed until well past midnight while Rader remained in the bedroom unnoticed. He waited for her to go to sleep, then came out of the closet and strangled her to death. He then took the body to his church's basement where he snapped several pictures of her in various poses before dumping her body in a ditch.

He was never a suspect for this crime and once again, he stopped killing until the following year. On September 16th, 1986 he knocked on the door at the home of Vicki Wegerle, twenty-eight, a young mother of two children, with the pretext of phones being out in the area and he needed to check hers. She let him in as he looked the part, hardhat and all. Once inside he told her that he was going to tie her up, and led her to the bedroom where he bound her using ropes and then strangled her with a pantyhose. He took off in her car just as her husband was coming around the corner. The husband, seeing his car being driven away, entered the house and found his wife. He called 911 but she died on the way to the hospital. The BTK Killer once again was never a suspect. Unfortunately when a spouse is killed, the other is always a person of interest, and although Bill Wegerle was never charged, until the BTK Killer was captured many years later, there was always suspicion hanging over his head. In my opinion, this is quite sad, as he already had enough to cope with. *Author's note: After researching so many crimes and writing several true-crime books, I have noticed a great deal of injustice in our system – as I've pointed out previously.*

Dennis Rader never killed for another five years, which happened to be his last known victim. On January 19th, 1991, Dolores Davis, 62, was reading in bed when she heard a glass break in her sliding backdoor. When she came out to investigate the noise, Rader was there pointing a gun at her. He took her to the bedroom and strangled her; brought the body out to the truck of her car, dumped her body out by the lake, returned the car and went home.

Over the next fourteen years, Rader supposedly never killed again. He was active in his community on various committees and boards, and involved on the board at the Christ Lutheran Church in Wichita. But in 2004 and 2005 he began sending messages and packages with evidence in it from past crimes to the police, taunting them, letting them know the BTK was still alive. His last package, actually the 11th package, was a floppy disc, letter, and some jewelry he sent to KSAS-TV on February 16th, 2005.

This last package proved to be sloppy on Rader's part. He thought he'd erased everything on the disc except the letter, but erasing a disc will not cut it; if you want to truly delete all information from a disc, you have to format it. So, when the investigators analyzed the disc, on it was software from the church, as well as the name, "Dennis." The detectives drove by Rader's house after doing an internet search and finding out that Dennis Rader was the president of the Christ Lutheran Church. They did not want to spook him, and very secretly obtained a warrant for DNA sampling. The results were startling yet exciting: they matched semen from several crime scenes. The police now conclusively knew the identity of the BTK Killer.

On February 25th, 2005, with a warrant in hand, police arrested Dennis

Rader as he was leaving his office to go home for lunch. He would spend the next thirty hours confessing to all his crimes. He pleaded guilty to the ten murders and on August 18th, 2005, he was sentenced to one hundred and seventy five – yep, 175 years in prison – but he is eligible for parole in the year 2180. I guess he will be old when he gets out. He currently resides at the El Dorado Correctional Facility in Kansas.

Chapter 31
David Berkowitz
Victims (13)

The Son of Sam

Richard David Falco was born on May 9th, 1953 in Brooklyn, New York, to Tony Falco and Betty Broder, who were separated at the time. His real father, however, was a man named Joseph Kleinman, as his mother had had an affair while she was married. The baby's mother put him up for adoption right away and he was legally adopted by Nathan and Pearl Berkowitz, who named their new son, David.

At eighteen years old, Berkowitz enlisted with the Army and served stateside and in South Korea until he was discharged three years later. As his adopted mother died when he was thirteen, he decided that twenty-one was a good time to search for his real mother. When he found her, she told him the details of his illegitimate birth, which upset him. After that, Berkowitz stayed away from his birth mother, but continued to have a relationship with his half sister, Roslyn.

Berkowitz was twenty-three when he started killing for reasons unknown. On July 29th, 1976, Rose and Mike Lauria and their daughter Donna, eighteen, and her friend, Jody Valenti, age nineteen, arrived home after midnight after a night out. They were just getting out of their car when Donna noticed a man rushing up to them. He pulled a handgun out of a paper bag, shot Donna in the chest and hit Jody in the leg. The shooter then quickly ran off. Donna's shot to the chest killed her instantly. The man was later described to police as being in his mid-thirties, almost six foot tall, about 160 pounds, with short, curly dark hair.

The police believed at the time that it was an attempted mob hit as the father, Mike Lauria, was with a teamsters union, or that it was gang related violence, common in New York at the time. They did discover through ballistics that the gun was a .44 Charter Arms Bulldog revolver. Just a few months later on October 23rd, 1976, there was another shooting. Around 1:30 a.m., Rosemary Keenan, thirty-eight, and Carl Denaro, twenty-five, were parked in Keenan's car in a secluded area in Queens when their windows exploded. Someone was shooting at them and she took off in the car. Both were bleeding and injured. However, neither of them were killed. Carl had to have surgery and required a metal plate in his head. They never saw the gunman. A police investigation was conducted thoroughly as Rosemary was the daughter of an NYPD police detective.

Police, however, had nothing to go on, and the .44 bullets that were removed from the car were too damaged to do any comparisons.

Just one month later, Joanne Lomino, eighteen, and Donna DeMasi, sixteen, were walking home from a movie on November 26th, 1976 when a man approached them. He drew a revolver and shot both of them, but both survived. Joanne is now a paraplegic. Donna was not permanently severely injured. Besides the two girls, another witness described the man as close to six-foot tall, slim, about 160 pounds, with dirty blond straight hair wearing a long coat that looked to be military.

John Diel, thirty, and Christine Freund, twenty-six, were recently engaged. On January 30th, 1977, they went to see the new release of the movie, Rocky. When they got into their car, someone shot through the window, killing Christine. John, however, managed to drive away with minor injuries. He never even got a glimpse of the shooter. As ballistics verified that the bullets came from a .44 Bulldog caliber, police made the connection with earlier shootings and suspected they had a serial killer on their hands.

Just two months later in Virginia on March 8th, 1977, Virginia Voskerichian, nineteen, was shot in the head on her own street. Just as she was shot, a resident came around the corner and almost collided with a young boy whom she described as about eighteen years old, short and tubby. The young boy said, "Oh, Jesus," and ran off. However, another witness saw the chubby teenager, but also saw another man who resembled the description of the man the media accused of other killings. Berkowitz later said that he was there, but he designed the shooting to throw off the police by changing his MO.

On March 10th, 1977, the Mayor of New York City, Abraham Beame, and the NYPD, announced that the same .44 was used to kill Virginia as was the previous murders, and added that a task force was now set up: Operation Omega, led by Deputy Inspector Tim Dowd and a force of over three hundred officers dedicated solely to the purpose of catching the suspect.

On the morning of April 17th, 1977, Valentina Suriani, eighteen, and Alexander Esau, twenty, were killed in their home at about 3a.m. Police discovered a hand written letter at the crime scene addressed to Captain Joseph Borrelli of the NYPD. The letter below is the actual words with errors intact:

"I am deeply hurt by your calling me a women hater. I am not. But I am a monster. I am the "Son of Sam." I am a little "brat." When father Sam gets drunk he gets mean. He beats his family. Sometimes he ties me up to the back of the house. Other times he locks me in the garage. Sam loves to drink blood. "Go out and kill" commands father Sam. Behind our house some rest. Mostly young — raped and slaughtered — their blood drained — just bones now. Papa Sam keeps me locked in the attic, too. I can't get out but I look out the attic window and watch the world go by. I feel like an outsider. I am on a different wave length then everybody else — programmed too kill. However, to stop me you must kill me. Attention all police:

Shoot me first — shoot to kill or else. Keep out of my way or you will die! Papa Sam is old now. He needs some blood to preserve his youth. He has had too many heart attacks. Too many heart attacks. "Ugh, me hoot it urts sonny boy." I miss my pretty princess most of all. She's resting in our ladies house but I'll see her soon. I am the "Monster" — "Beelzebub" — the "Chubby Behemouth." I love to hunt. Prowling the streets looking for fair game — tasty meat. The wemon of Queens are z prettyist of all. I must be the water they drink. I live for the hunt — my life. Blood for papa. Mr. Borrelli, sir, I dont want to kill anymore no sir, no more but I must, "honour thy father." I want to make love to the world. I love people. I don't belong on Earth. Return me to yahoos. To the people of Queens, I love you. And I wa want to wish all of you a happy Easter. May God bless you in this life and in the next and for now I say goodbye and goodnight. Police — Let me haunt you with these words; I'll be back! I'll be back! To be interrpreted as — bang, bang, bang, bank, bang — ugh!! Yours in murder Mr. Monster"

On May 30th, 1977, Jimmy Breslin, a Columnist with the New York Daily News received a hand written letter from someone who claimed to be the .44 shooter. On the reverse of the envelope in a precise centered quatrain:

"Blood and Family/Darkness and Death/Absolute Depravity/.44"

The letter is as follows, with errors, as it was written:

"Hello from the gutters of N.Y.C. which are filled with dog manure, vomit, stale wine, urine and blood. Hello from the sewers of N.Y.C. which swallow up these delicacies when they are washed away by the sweeper trucks. Hello from the cracks in the sidewalks of N.Y.C. and from the ants that dwell in these cracks and feed in the dried blood of the dead that has settled into the cracks. J.B., I'm just dropping you a line to let you know that I appreciate your interest in those recent and horrendous .44 killings. I also want to tell you that I read your column daily and I find it quite informative. Tell me Jim, what will you have for July twenty-ninth? You can forget about me if you like because I don't care for publicity. However you must not forget Donna Lauria and you cannot let the people forget her either. She was a very, very sweet girl but Sam's a thirsty lad and he won't let me stop killing until he gets his fill of blood. Mr. Breslin, sir, don't think that because you haven't heard from me for a while that I went to sleep. No, rather, I am still here. Like a spirit roaming the night. Thirsty, hungry, seldom stopping to rest; anxious to please Sam. I love my work. Now, the void has been filled. Perhaps we shall meet face to face someday or perhaps I will be blown away by cops with smoking . 38's. Whatever, if I shall be fortunate enough to meet you I will tell you all about Sam if you like and I will introduce you to him. His name is "Sam the terrible." Not knowing the what the future holds I shall say farewell and I will see you at the next job. Or should I say you will see my handiwork at the next job? Remember Ms. Lauria. Thank you. In their blood and from the gutter "Sam's creation" .44 Here are some names to help you along. Forward them to the inspector for use by N.C.I.C. "The Duke of Death" "The Wicked King

Wicker" "The Twenty Two Disciples of Hell" "John 'Wheaties' – Rapist and Suffocator of Young Girls. PS: Please inform all the detectives working the slaying to remain. P.S: JB, Please inform all the detectives working the case that I wish them the best of luck. "Keep 'em digging, drive on, think positive, get off your butts, knock on coffins, etc." Upon my capture I promise to buy all the guys working the case a new pair of shoes if I can get up the money. Son of Sam"

By this time, police were concentrating on the Bronx and Queens areas, looking for a suspect in the shootings, but the next victims were in Brooklyn. Robert Violante, twenty, and his girlfriend Stacy Moskowitz, twenty, were in his car, parked near a city park when a man approached and fired through the passenger side window, shooting both of them in the head. Stacy died instantly and Robert was seriously injured and left nearly blind. The shooting occurred around 2:30 a.m. on July 31st, 1977.

The police got a break after this shooting as there were several witnesses, each describing the man as previously described; however, they all said it looked like the man had been wearing a dark wig. But the big break came when one female witness got a glimpse of his partial license plate number, either 4 GUR or 4 GVR. Other witnesses saw a man driving off in a hurry with his lights off and described the car as a yellow Volkswagen. Another witness said she'd seen a man walking away from the shooting while others were walking towards it to assist the victims. She would later identify him in a lineup.

After the last shooting, a woman by the name of Cacilia Davis, who happened to live close to the crime scene, saw a man removing a parking ticket from his yellow car, which had been parked to close to a fire hydrant. Two days later, she contacted the police who checked into the ticket, figuring the man who owned the car was a witness, not a suspect. It was not until seven days later that Detective James Justis of the NYPD called Yonkers police to ask them to set up an interview with Berkowitz, still thinking he was a witness.

On August 10th, 1977, a police officer

went to Berkowitz's house to set up a meeting. While he was walking up the driveway, he happened to look inside the car, and noticed a rifle in the backseat. The officer opened the door (without a search warrant) and found a duffel bag with ammunition, a letter to the task force, and maps of the crime scenes. He called for backup and when Berkowitz came out of his apartment at about 10 a.m., police arrested him, and found a .44 Bulldog handgun on his person. The Son of Sam's first words were, "You got me. What took you so long?"

That same day, Mayor Beame of New York City made a statement to the media and public saying, "The people of the City of New York can rest easy. The police have captured a man whom they believe to be the Son of Sam."

The search of Berkowitz's car was later justified as the officer had seen a rifle in the car. In the state of New York, that was justifiable reasoning to engage in a further search, which was a lucky break for the DA. Berkowitz said he would plead guilty on all charges and confess to being the Son of Sam killer provided that he would not get the death penalty. A plea was accepted.

For his murders, on June 12th, 1978, Berkowitz was sentenced to a term of 365 years. Of course he became a born again Christian the following year in prison. Currently, Berkowitz lives in Sullivan Correctional Facility in Fallsburg, New York. His official website is maintained on his behalf by a church group as he is not allowed access to a computer. If you are interested, here is a link to his website: http://www.ariseandshine.org/index.html

Chapter 32
John Allen Muhammad
and Lee Malvo
Victims (24)

The D.C. Snipers

Born as John Allen Williams on December 31st, 1960, in Baton Rouge, Louisiana, Williams enlisted in the Louisiana Army National Guard in 1979 and, after seven years of service, volunteered for active duty in 1986.

In 1987, Williams joined the Nation of

Islam. While in the Army, he was trained as a mechanic, truck driver, and specialist metalworker. He qualified with the Army's standard infantry rifle the M16, earning the Expert Rifleman's Badge. This rating is the Army's highest of three levels of marksmanship for a basic soldier. He was discharged from military service following the Gulf War, as a sergeant, in 1994.

As a member of the Nation of Islam, "Muhammad" helped provide security for the Million Man March in 1995 – Nation of Islam leader Louis Farrakhan has publicly distanced himself and his organization from Muhammad's crimes. Muhammad kidnapped his children and brought them to Antigua around 1999, apparently engaging in credit card and immigration document fraud activities. It was during this time that he became close with Lee Boyd Malvo, who later acted as his partner in the killings. Williams changed his name to John Allen Muhammad in October 2001.

Lee Boyd Malvo was born February 18th, 1985, in Kingston, Jamaica to Leslie Malvo, a mason, and Una James, a seamstress. Lee's parents never married and separated when he was a toddler. Leslie Malvo rarely saw his son after that and subsequently his mother raised Lee by herself and was quite poor. Lee and his mother left Jamaica when he was about fourteen years old, moving to the island of Antigua.

Una James eventually left Antigua for Fort Myers, Florida, travelling on false documents she'd purchased after meeting Muhammad, where she lived illegally. She left Lee with Muhammad. Her son was supposed to join her a few months later.

In 2001, Muhammad, who claimed Malvo as being his stepson, moved to Bellingham, Washington, and tried to enroll him and his three children in a school. He was caught by the authorities, however, who returned the three children to their mother. Malvo was reunited briefly with his mother in Miami, but they were arrested by the Border Patrol. Malvo was released on a $1,500 bond the next year and met up with Muhammad again.

While the two of them lived at a homeless shelter in Bellingham, Malvo enrolled in high school but made no friends. On a trip to Tacoma, Washington, they tried to kill one of his ex-wife's friends, but ended up killing her niece instead. After a trip to Muhammad's relatives in Louisiana, the two bought a 1990 Chevy Caprice and began a series of robberies and shootings in Louisiana, Alabama, and Maryland.

The Chevy Caprice became a rolling sniper's nest. During this time, they are believed to have committed another murder – and seven more by the end of October. Malvo shoplifted a Bushmaster XM-15 rifle from a firearms shop. Muhammad took up target practice at a gun range nearby.

The massive investigation into the sniper attacks was led by the Montgomery County Police Department, and headed by Chief Charles Moose, with the F.B.I. and many other law enforcement agencies playing a supporting role. Chief Moose had specifically requested the help of the F.B.I. to try to catch the sniper.

On October 2nd, 2002, the duo began what became a full-scale spree of random shootings across Virginia, Maryland, and

D.C. Over the course of twenty-three days they shot and killed ten people and injured an additional three. They were actually pulled over at one point, but since Muhammad had no outstanding warrants, were let go.

At the peak of the rampage, people were afraid to leave their houses. The F.B.I. had nearly 400 Agents assigned to the investigation, including teams of new agents in training who were working the toll-free hotline.

The following is a timeline of murders committed during the shooting spree:

October 2nd: James Martin, fifty-five, killed while crossing a parking lot in Wheaton, Maryland

October 3rd: Five more murders: four in Maryland and one in D.C.: James Buchanan, thirty-nine; Premkumar Walekar, fifty-four; Sarah Ramos, thirty-four; Lori Ann Lewis-Rivera, twenty-five; and Pascal Charlot, seventy-two.

October 4th: Caroline Seawell, forty-three, wounded while loading her van at Spotsylvania Mall.

October 7th: Iran Brown, thirteen,

wounded at a school in Bowie, Maryland.

October 9th: Dean Meyers, fifty-three, murdered near Manassas, Virginia, while pumping gas.

October 11th: Kenneth Bridges, fifty-three, shot dead near Fredericksburg, Virginia, while pumping gas,

October 14th: F.B.I. Analyst Linda Franklin, forty-seven, killed near Falls Church, Virginia.

October 19th: Jeffrey Hopper, thirty-seven, wounded outside a steakhouse in Ashland, Virginia.

October 22nd: Conrad Johnson, thirty-five – the final victim – killed in Aspen Hill, Maryland.

Early in the morning of October 24th, their dark blue 1990 Chevy Caprice, which had been widely publicized on the news, was spotted at a rest-stop parking-lot off I-70 in Maryland. Within the hour, law enforcement swarmed the scene, setting up a perimeter to check out any movements and make sure there was no way to escape. They found both of the killers asleep inside the car.

What the F.B.I. and other police forces

found in the car was both revealing and shocking. The car had a hole cut in the trunk near the license plate so that shots could be fired from within the vehicle. The Caprice was, in effect, a rolling sniper's nest.

The execution for Muhammad was scheduled for November 10th, 2009, and although there was an appeal, it was denied. Muhammad was put to death by lethal injection. He declined to make a final statement.

Malvo pled guilty to six murders in Maryland while being interviewed, and confessed to more in other states while testifying against Muhammad. Malvo was sentenced to six consecutive life terms without the possibility of parole.

Chapter 33
Tsutomu Miyazaki
(Victims (4+)

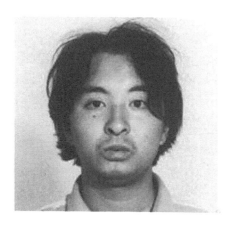

The Little Girl Murderer

Tsutomu Miyazaki was born on August 21st, 1962 in Tokyo, Japan. Born prematurely, he had deformed hands which were permanently bent and fused directly to the wrists, necessitating him to move his entire forearm in order to rotate the hand. Due to his deformity, he was not accepted when he attended Itsukaichi

Elementary School, and consequently kept to himself. Although he was originally a star student, his grades at Meidai Nakano High School dropped dramatically. He had a class rank of 40 out of 56 and did not receive the customary admission to Meiji University. Instead of studying English and becoming a teacher as he had originally intended, he attended a local junior college, where he studied to become a photo technician.

In 1988 and 1989 Miyazaki mutilated and killed four girls between the ages of four and seven, sexually molesting their corpses. He drank the blood of one victim and ate a part of her hand. These crimes which, prior to Miyazaki's apprehension and trial, were named, 'The Little Girl Murders,' were later known as the Tokyo/Saitama Serial Kidnappings. The murders of the little girls shocked Saitama Prefecture, which had few crimes against children. During the day, Miyazaki was a mild-mannered employee; outside of work he randomly selected children to kill. He terrorized the families of his victims, sending them letters which recounted, in graphic detail, what he had done to their children. To the family of victim Erika Nanba, Miyazaki sent a morbid postcard assembled using words cut out of magazines: "Erika. Cold. Cough. Throat. Rest. Death."

He allowed the corpse of his first victim, Mari Konno, age four, to decompose in the hills near his home, then he chopped off her hands and feet, which he kept in his closet, and were recovered upon his arrest. He burnt her remaining bones in his furnace, ground them into powder, and sent them to her family in a box along with several of her teeth, photos of her clothes, and a postcard reading: "Mari. Cremated. Bones. Investigate. Prove."

Police found that the families of the victims had something else in common: all were bothered by silent, annoying phone calls. If they did not pick up the phone, it would sometimes ring for twenty minutes.

On July 23rd, 1989, Miyazaki attempted to insert a zoom lens into the vagina of a grade school-aged girl in a park near her home and was attacked by the girl's grandfather. After fleeing naked on foot, Miyazaki eventually returned to the park to retrieve his car, at which point he was promptly arrested by police who had responded to a call by the grandfather.

A search of Miyazaki's two-room bungalow turned up a collection of 5,763 videotapes, some containing Slasher films, later used as reasoning for his crimes.

Among the tapes police found footage and pictures of his victims. He was also reported to be a fan of horror films, having an extensive collection, including the fourth film of the Guinea Pig film series (Mermaid in a Manhole). Miyazaki, who retained a perpetually calm and collected demeanor during his trial, appeared indifferent to his capture.

Miyazaki's father refused to pay for his son's legal defense. The trial began on March 30th, 1990. Often talking nonsense, he blamed his violence on 'Rat Man,' an alter ego whom Miyazaki claimed forced him to kill. He spent a great deal of the trial drawing 'Rat Man' in cartoon form. Believed to be insane, Miyazaki remained incarcerated throughout the 1990s while

Saitama Prefecture put him through a battery of psychiatric evaluations.

Teams of psychiatrists from Tokyo University diagnosed him as suffering from dissociative identity disorder (multiple personalities) or extreme schizophrenia. The Tokyo District Court, however, judged him still aware of the gravity and consequences of his crimes, and therefore accountable. He was sentenced to death on April 14th, 1997. His death sentence was upheld by the Tokyo High Court, on June 28th, 2001, and the Supreme Court of Justice on January 17th, 2006.

Judge Kunio Hatoyama signed his death warrant. Miyazaki was hanged on June 17th, 2008.

Chapter 34
Andrei Chikatilo
Victims (52)

The Butcher of Rostov

Andrei Chikatilo was born on October 16th, 1936, in the village of Yablochnoye in modern Sumy Oblast of the Ukrainian. At the time, Ukrainian farmers were forced to hand in their entire crop for statewide distribution. Mass starvation ran rampant throughout the Ukraine and reports of cannibalism soared. Chikatilo's mother, Anna, told him that his older brother, Stepan, had been kidnapped and cannibalized by starving neighbors, although it has never been independently established whether this actually happened. Chikatilo was a chronic bed wetter and was berated and beaten by his mother for each offense.

When the Soviet Union entered World War II, his father, Roman, was drafted into the Red Army and subsequently taken prisoner after being wounded in combat. During the war, Chikatilo witnessed some of the effects of Germany's blitzkrieg warfare, which both frightened and excited him. On one occasion, Chikatilo and his mother were forced to watch their hut burn to the ground. In 1943, while Chikatilo's father was at the front, his mother gave birth to a baby girl, Tatyana. In 1949, Chikatilo's father, who had been freed by the Americans, returned home. Instead of being rewarded for his war service, he was branded a traitor for surrendering to the Germans.

Chikatilo was shy as a child and developed a passion for reading. By his teens, he was an avid reader of Communist literature, and was appointed chairperson of the pupils' Communist committee at his school. Throughout his childhood and adolescence, he was consistently a target for bullying by other students. During adolescence, he discovered that he suffered from chronic impotence, aggravating his social awkwardness and self-hatred. Chikatilo was shy in the company of females. His only sexual experience as a teenager was when he was seventeen. He jumped on an eleven-year-old friend of his younger sister and wrestled her to the ground, ejaculating as the girl struggled in his grasp.

Between 1957 and 1960, Chikatilo performed his compulsory military service, and in 1963, married a woman to whom he was introduced by his younger sister. The couple had a son and a daughter. Chikatilo later claimed that his marital sex life was minimal and that, after his wife understood that he was unable to maintain an erection, he and his wife agreed that in order for her to conceive, he would ejaculate externally and push his semen inside her vagina with his fingers. *YUCK*!

On December 22nd, 1978, Chikatilo lured Yelena Zakotnova, nine years old, to an old house he had secretly purchased, and tried to rape her. He failed to achieve an erection, however, and when the girl struggled he choked her to death and stabbed her body, ejaculating in the process of knifing the little girl. Chikatilo then dumped her body in a nearby river. Spots of the girl's blood were found in the snow near Chikatilo's house, and a witness gave police a detailed description of a man closely resembling Chikatilo whom she had seen the talking with the girl at the bus stop where she had last been seen alive.

However, Alexsandr Kravchenko, twenty-five, who, as a teenager, had served a jail sentence for the rape and murder of a teenage girl, was arrested for this murder and subsequently confessed to the killing. He was tried for the murder in 1979. At his trial, Kravchenko retracted his confession and maintained his innocence, stating his confession had been obtained under extreme duress.

Despite his retraction, Kravchenko was convicted of the murder and sentenced to fifteen years in prison. Under demands from the victim's relatives, Kravchenko was retried and eventually executed for the murder of Yelena Zakotnova in July, 1983, although he proclaimed his innocence. Following Zakotnova's murder, Chikatilo was able to achieve sexual arousal and orgasm only through stabbing and slashing women and children to death, and he later claimed that the urge to relive the experience had plagued him.

Chikatilo began his career as a teacher of Russian language and literature in Novoshakhtinsk. His career as a teacher ended, however, in March of 1981, after several complaints arose that he had molested several students of both sexes. Chikatilo eventually took a job as a supply clerk for a factory.

Chikatilo committed his next murder in September of 1981 when he again tried to have sex with Larisa Tkachenko, seventeen, in a forest near the Don River.

When Chikatilo failed to reach an erection, he became livid and battered and strangled her to death. As he had no knife, he mutilated her body with his teeth and a stick.

Then again, on June 12th, 1982, Chikatilo encountered Lyubov Biryuk, thirteen, walking home from a shopping trip in the village of Donskoi. Once the path both were taking together was shielded from the view of potential witnesses by bushes, Chikatilo pounced upon Biryuk, dragged her into nearby undergrowth, tore off her blue floral dress, and killed her by stabbing and slashing her to death. Following Biryuk's murder, Chikatilo no longer attempted to resist his homicidal urges. Between July and December, 1982, he killed a further six victims between the ages of nine and nineteen.

Chikatilo established a pattern of approaching children, runaways, and young vagrants at bus or railway stations, enticing them to a nearby forest or other secluded area, and killing them, usually by stabbing, slashing, and disemboweling the victim with a knife. Some victims, in addition to receiving a multitude of knife wounds, were also strangled, had their eyes gouged out, or battered to death. Chikatilo's adult female victims were often prostitutes or homeless women who could be lured to secluded areas with promises of alcohol or money. Chikatilo would typically attempt intercourse with these victims, but he would usually be unable to get an erection, which would again send him into a murderous fury, especially if the woman mocked his impotence. He would achieve orgasm only when he stabbed the victim to death.

Chikatilo did not kill again until June 1983, but he had killed five more times by September of that year. The accumulation of bodies and the similarities between the patterns of wounds inflicted on the victims forced the Soviet authorities to acknowledge that a serial killer was on the loose, and on September 6th, 1983, the public prosecutor of the USSR formally linked six of the murders thus far committed to the same killer.

A Moscow investigative team of police officers, headed by Major Mikhail

Fetisov, was sent to Rostov-on-Don to direct the investigation. Major Fetisov centered the investigations on the Shakhty area and assigned a specialist forensic analyst, Victor Burakov, to lead the investigation. Due to the absolute savagery of the murders, much of the police effort concentrated on homosexuals, known pedophiles, mentally ill citizens, and sex offenders, slowly working through all that were known and eliminating them from the investigation. Three known homosexuals and a convicted sex offender committed suicide because of the investigator's unsympathetic tactics. But as police obtained confessions from suspects, bodies continued to be discovered, proving that the suspects who had confessed could not be the killer the police were seeking.

In October of 1983, Chikatilo killed a nineteen-year-old prostitute and in December a fourteen-year-old pupil named Sergey Markov. In January and February of 1984, Chikatilo killed two women in Rostov's Aviators Park and on March 24th, lured Dmitry Ptashnikov, ten years old, away from a stamp kiosk in

Novoshakhtinsk. While walking with the boy, Chikatilo was seen by several witnesses who were able to give investigators a detailed description of the killer. When the boy's body was found three days later, police also discovered a footprint of the killer, as well as semen and saliva samples on the victim's clothes.

On May 25th, Chikatilo killed a young woman, Tatyana Petrosyan, and her eleven-year-old daughter, Svetlana, in a wooded area outside Shakhty. Tatyana had known Chikatilo for several years prior to her murder. By July 19th, he had killed three more young women between the ages of nineteen and twenty-two, and a boy of only thirteen.

Chikatilo was fired in 1984 from his work as a supply clerk for theft. The allegation had been filed against Chikatilo the previous February and he had been asked to leave quietly, but had refused to do so as he had disapproved of the charges. Chikatilo found another job as a supply clerk in Rostov and in early August he killed Natalya Golosovskaya, sixteen, in Aviators Park, and the next day another girl only seventeen, dumping her body on the banks of the Don River before flying to the Uzbekistan capital of Tashkent on a business trip.

By the time Chikatilo returned to Rostov in mid-August, he had killed another young woman and a twelve-year-old girl. Within two weeks, an eleven year-old boy had been found strangled and castrated with his eyes gouged out in Rostov before a young librarian, Irina Luchinskaya, was killed in Rostov's Aviators Park in early September. Exactly one week after his fifteenth killing of the year, Chikatilo was observed by an undercover detective attempting to lure young women away from a Rostov bus station. He was arrested and held. A search of his belongings revealed a knife and rope. He was also discovered to be under investigation for minor theft at one of his former employers, which gave the investigators the legal right to hold him for a prolonged period. Chikatilo's dubious background was uncovered, and his physical description matched the description of the man seen with Dmitry

Ptashnikov in March. These factors alone did not provide enough evidence to convict him of the murders. He was, however, found guilty of theft of property from his previous employer and sentenced to one year in prison, but was freed on December 12th, 1984 after serving only three months.

Following the September 6th murder of Irina Luchinskaya, no further bodies were found bearing the trademark mutilation of Chikatilo's murders. Investigators in Rostov theorized that the unknown killer might have moved to another part of the Soviet Union and continued killing there. The Rostov police sent bulletins to all forces throughout the Soviet Union, describing the pattern of wounds their unknown killer inflicted upon his victims, and requested feedback from any police force that had discovered victims with wounds matching those upon the victims found in the Rostov Oblast. The response was negative.

Upon his release from jail, Chikatilo found new work in Novocherkassk and kept a low profile. He did not kill again until seven months after getting out of jail when he murdered a young woman close to Domodedovo Airport, near Moscow. One month later, in August, Chikatilo killed another woman in Shakhty. Both victims were linked to the hunt for the killer as the same modus operandi was used in the killings.

In November of 1985, a special procurator named Issa Kostoyev was appointed to supervise the investigation of the serial killer. The known murders around Rostov were carefully re-investigated and police began questioning known sex offenders again. The following month, the militia and Voluntary People's Druzhina renewed the patrolling of railway stations around Rostov. The police also took the step of consulting a psychiatrist, Dr. Alexandr Bukhanovsky, the first such consultation in a serial killer investigation in the Soviet Union. Bukhanovsky produced a sixty-five page psychological profile of the unknown killer for the investigators, describing the killer as a man between forty-five and fifty years old who was of average intelligence, likely to be married or had previously been married, but also a sadist who could achieve sexual arousal only by seeing his victims suffer. Bukhanovsky also argued that because many of the killings had occurred on weekdays near mass transportation and across the entire Rostov Oblast, the killer's work required him to travel regularly and, based upon the actual days of the week when the killings had occurred, the killer was most likely tied to a production schedule.

Chikatilo followed the investigation carefully, reading newspaper reports about the manhunt for the killer, and kept his homicidal urges under control. Throughout 1986 he is not known to have committed any murders. That did not last long.

In 1987, Chikatilo killed three more times. On each occasion he killed while on a business trip far away from the Rostov Oblast, and none of those murders were linked to the manhunt in Rostov. Chikatilo's committed his first murder of 1987 in May when he killed a thirteen-year-old boy named Oleg Makarenkov in Revda. In July, he killed another boy in Zaporozhye, and a third in Leningrad in September. In 1988,

Chikatilo killed three times, murdering an unidentified woman in Krasny-Sulin in April, and two boys in May and July. His first killing bore wounds similar to those inflicted on the victims linked to the manhunt killed between 1982 and 1985, but as the woman had been killed with a slab of concrete, investigators were unsure whether or not to link the murder to the investigation. In May of the same year, Chikatilo killed a nine-year-old boy in Ilovaisk, Ukraine. The boy's wounds left no doubt that the killer had struck again; this murder was linked to the manhunt. On July 14th, Chikatilo killed a fifteen-year old boy named Yevgeny Muratov at Donleskhoz station near Shakhty. Muratov's murder was also linked to the investigation, although his body was not found until April, 1989.

Chikatilo did not kill again for another year, not until March 8th, 1989, when he killed a sixteen-year-old girl in his daughter's vacant apartment. He dismembered her body and hid the remains in a sewer. As the victim had been dismembered, police did not link her murder to the investigation. Between May and August, Chikatilo killed a further four victims, three of whom were killed in Rostov and Shakhty, although only two of the victims were linked to the killer.

On January 14th, 1990, Chikatilo killed an eleven-year-old boy in Shakhty. On March 7th, he killed a ten-year old boy named Yaroslav Makarov in Rostov Botanical Gardens. The eviscerated body was found the following day. On March 11th, the leaders of the investigation, headed by Mikhail Fetisov, held a meeting to discuss progress made in the hunt for the killer. Fetisov was under intense pressure from the public, the press, and the Ministry of the Interior in Moscow, to solve the case. The intensity of the manhunt in the years up to 1984 had receded a degree between 1985 and 1987, when only two victims had been conclusively linked to the killer, both of them in 1985.

But by March 1990, six further victims had been linked to the serial killer. Fetisov had noted laxity in some areas of the investigation, and warned that people would be fired if the killer was not caught soon. Chikatilo killed three further victims by August. On April 4th, he killed a thirty-one year old woman in woodland near Donleskhoz station; on July 28th, he lured a thirteen year old boy away from a Rostov train station and killed him in Rostov Botanical Gardens; and on August 14th, he killed an eleven year old boy in the reeds near Novocherkassk beach.

Police deployed a very visible 360 men at all the stations in the Rostov Oblast, and positioned undercover officers at the three smallest stations: Kirpichnaya, Donleskhoz, and Lesoste. These were the routes through the Oblast where the killer had struck most frequently. Police hoped to force the killer to strike at one of these three stations. The operation was implemented on October 27th, 1990, but, on October 30th, police found the body of a sixteen-year-old boy named Vadim Gromov at Donleskhoz Station. Gromov, however, had been killed on October 17th, ten days before the start of the initiative. The same day Gromov's body was found, Chikatilo lured another sixteen year-old boy, Viktor

Tishchenko, off a train at Kirpichnaya Station, a different station under surveillance from undercover police, and killed him in a nearby forest.

Just six days later, Chikatilo killed and mutilated a twenty-two year-old woman named Svetlana Korostik in a woodland near Donleskhoz Station. While leaving the crime scene, an undercover officer spotted him approach a well and wash his hands and face. When Chikatilo approached the station, the undercover officer noted that his coat had grass and soil stains on the elbows, and Chikatilo had a small red smear on his cheek. To the officer, he looked suspicious. The only reason people entered woodland near the station at that time of year was to gather wild mushrooms, a popular pastime in Russia. Chikatilo, however, was not dressed like a typical forest hiker. He was wearing more formal attire. Moreover, he had a nylon sports bag, which was not suitable for carrying mushrooms.

The undercover police officer stopped Chikatilo and checked his papers, but had no formal reason to arrest him.

When the police officer returned to his office, he filed a routine report, containing the name of the person he had stopped at the train station. On November 13th, Korostik's body was found. Police summoned the officer in charge of surveillance at Donleskhoz Station and examined the reports of all men stopped and questioned in the previous week. Chikatilo's name was among those reports, and his name was familiar to several officers involved in the case, as he had been questioned in 1984 and placed upon a 1987 suspect list that had been compiled and distributed throughout the Soviet Union. Upon checking with Chikatilo's present and previous employers, investigators were able to place Chikatilo in various towns and cities at times when several victims linked to the investigation had been killed.

Former colleagues from Chikatilo's teaching days informed investigators that Chikatilo had been forced to resign from his teaching position due to complaints of sexual assault from several pupils. Police placed Chikatilo under surveillance on

November 14th. In several instances, particularly on trains or buses, he was observed approaching lone young women or children and engaging them in conversation. If the woman or child broke off the conversation, Chikatilo would wait a few minutes and then seek another conversation partner. On November 20th, after six days of surveillance, Chikatilo left his house with a one-gallon flask of beer and wandered around Novocherkassk attempting to make contact with children. Upon exiting a cafe, Chikatilo was arrested by four plainclothes police officers.

After being arrested, Chikatilo gave a statement claiming that the police were mistaken, and complained that he had also been arrested in 1984 for the same series of murders. A strip search revealed that one of Chikatilo's fingers had a flesh wound, and medical examiners concluded the wound was, in fact, from a human bite. Chikatilo's second to last victim was a physically strong sixteen year-old youth. At the crime scene, the police had found numerous signs of a ferocious physical struggle between the victim and his murderer. Although a finger bone was found to be broken and his fingernail had been bitten off, Chikatilo had never sought medical treatment for the wound. A search of Chikatilo's belongings revealed that he had been in possession of a folding knife at the time of his arrest. Chikatilo was placed in a cell inside the KGB headquarters in Rostov with a police informant who was instructed to engage Chikatilo in conversation and obtain any information he could from him.

The next day, the 21st of November, formal questioning of Chikatilo was begun by Issa Kostoyev. The police's strategy to elicit a confession from Chikatilo was to lead him to believe that he was a very sick man in need of medical help. This was done in order to give Chikatilo hope that, if he confessed, he would not be prosecuted by reason of insanity. Police knew their case against Chikatilo was largely circumstantial, and under Soviet law they had ten days in which they could legally hold a suspect before they either had to charge him or release him. Throughout the questioning, Chikatilo repeatedly denied that he had committed the murders, although he did confess to molesting his pupils during his career as a teacher.

On November 29th, at the request of Burakov and Fetisov, Dr. Aleksandr Bukhanovsky, the psychiatrist who had written the 1985 psychological profile of the then-unknown killer for the investigators, was invited to assist in the questioning of the suspect. Bukhanovsky read extracts from his sixty-five page psychological profile to Chikatilo. Within two hours, Chikatilo confessed to the thirty-six murders that police had linked to the killer. On November 30th, he was formally charged with each of these thirty-six murders, all of which had been committed between June of 1982 and November of 1990.

Chikatilo also confessed to a further twenty killings which had not been connected to him as the murders had been committed outside the Rostov Oblast, and the bodies had not been found. Chikatilo then led police to the body of Aleksey Khobotov, a boy he had confessed to killing in 1989, and who he had buried in woodland near a Shakhty cemetery, proving unequivocally that he was the killer. He later led investigators to the bodies of two other victims he had confessed to killing. Three of the fifty-six victims Chikatilo confessed to killing could not be found or identified, hence Chikatilo was charged with killing fifty-three women and children between 1978 and 1990.

Chikatilo stood trial in Rostov on April 14th, 1992. It was necessary to keep him in an iron cage in a corner of the courtroom to protect him from attack by the many hysterical and enraged relatives of his victims. Relatives of victims regularly shouted threats and insults to Chikatilo throughout the trial, demanding that authorities release him so that they could kill him themselves. Each murder was discussed individually and, on several occasions, relatives broke down in tears when details of their relatives' murder were revealed; some even fainted.

Chikatilo regularly interrupted the trial, exposing himself, singing, and refusing to answer questions put to him by the judge. He was regularly removed from the courtroom for interrupting the proceedings. In July of 1992, Chikatilo demanded that the judge be replaced for making too many rash remarks about his guilt. His defense counsel backed the claim.

The judge looked to the prosecutor, and the prosecutor backed the defense's judgment, stating that the judge had indeed made too many such remarks. The judge ruled the prosecutor be replaced instead.

On October 15th, Chikatilo was found guilty of fifty-two of the fifty-three murders and sentenced to death for each offense. Chikatilo kicked his bench across his cage when he heard the verdict, and began shouting abuse. He was offered a final chance to make a speech in response to the verdict, but remained silent. Upon passing final sentence, Judge Leonid Akhobzyanov made the following speech: "Taking into consideration the monstrous crimes he committed, this court has no alternative but to impose the only sentence that he deserves. I therefore sentence him to death."

On January 4th, 1994, Russian

President Boris Yeltsin refused a final appeal for clemency for Chikatilo, and ten days later he was taken to a soundproofed room in a Novocherkassk prison and executed with a single gunshot behind the right ear.

Chapter 35

Ottis Toole
and
Henry Lee Lucas

Ottis Toole (left) – The Devil's Child Killer (Victims 766)

Henry Lee Lucas (right) – The Confession Killer (Victims 766)

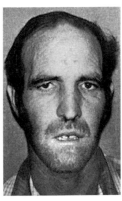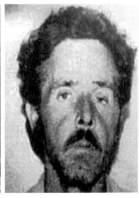

Ottis Toole was born on March 5th, 1947 in Jacksonville, Florida. As a child, he was a victim of sexual assault, molested by family and friends according to him. He claimed that his grandmother was a Satanist who exposed him to rituals, self-mutilation, and grave robbing, and called him the "Devil's Child." Now, before I begin, let me just say that this murderous duo was either composed of the two biggest exaggerators in history, or the worst serial killers the world has ever seen, with killings in the hundreds between them.

I would assume that all serial killers have some kind of mental illness. As for Toole, he was diagnosed with mild retardation: an IQ of only 75, dyslexia, illiteracy, ADHD, epilepsy, and he also suffered from grand mal seizures. Ottis Toole fits the classical marks in the making of a serial killer: he was a bed-wetter, an animal killer, an arsonist, got sexually excited by fire, and all this before he was a teenager. By the time he was thirteen years old he'd dropped out of school and was working as a male prostitute in drag. At a soup kitchen in 1976, Toole met Henry Lee Lucas and the two began a sexual relationship. They later claimed that while they were together they committed 108 murders with a cult called 'The Hands of Death.'

Henry Lee Lucas was born on August

23rd, 1936 in Blacksburg, Virginia, to an alcoholic father and an alcoholic/prostitute mother. Lucas is considered by law enforcement to be *the* worst serial killer in American history. His mother would often beat, abuse, and ignore him. When he was ten years old, he and his brother got into a fight and his brother stabbed him in the eye; his mother did not bother getting it treated and he ended up losing his sight in that eye.

Henry Lucas dropped out of elementary school in the 6th grade, ran away from home, and drifted around the state of Virginia. Lucas maintained that in the beginning, when he left home, he practiced bestiality and Zoosadism, and began committing minor thefts and burglaries around the state, for which he spent five years in prison: 1954 to 1959. In January of 1960, he got into a fight with his mother and stabbed her to death. He went to prison for another ten years and was released in 1970 as the prison was overcrowded. He drifted around the southern states working menial jobs and met Ottis Toole in 1976. They formed what they called the 'homosexual crime team,' and began a cross-country murder bender which left at least 108 people dead in their wake.

Ottis Toole was arrested in April, 1983 in Jacksonville, for burning down a church, and given a fifteen-year sentence. Two months later, in June, his partner in crime, Henry Lee Lucas, was arrested for unlawful possession of a firearm. It was then that Lucas began boasting about the murderous storm orchestrated by the two of them. Initially, Toole denied any involvement, but later began backing up Lucas's confessions.

A task force was established in June of 1983 called 'The Lucas Task Force.' Police had to verify scores of killings that Lucas had admitted to committing which had been previously thought to be unconnected. In one case, a woman had even been denied a large insurance settlement after her husband's death had been ruled a suicide, but once Lucas admitted to the killing of her husband – and could prove it – the insurance company paid her a settlement. The task force, including the Texas Rangers, was shocked at the number of names and files that were being collected and investigated. Lucas knew details in the files that only the killer would know. In another prison, Toole was spilling the same details, and more of his own individual crimes. In 1985, Toole and Lucas enjoyed a more laidback imprisonment, living in virtual comfort, purportedly receiving private meals and special accommodations in their prison cells because they were helping authorities close hundreds of cold cases. The police took them to various states, visiting the old crime scenes and burial sites of their many victims, all while enjoying a bit of sight-seeing, being outside their cells.

Toole was sentenced to six life sentences and he died on September 15th, 1996, at the age of forty-nine in his prison cell from liver failure. Nobody claimed his body and he was buried in a prison cemetery. Lucas also was sentenced to life so that authorities could try to gain more information about past crimes. Lucas died in prison from heart failure at age sixty-four on March 13th, 2001.

Case Closed? Not quite.

Adam Walsh

Young Adam Walsh was only six years old, an innocent little boy, when taken from this world by a monster on July 27th, 1981. It would be twenty-seven years before his mom and dad would know who killed him. On December 16th, 2008, police announced that Ottis Toole killed little Adam. Because of his son's murder, John Walsh became a campaigner for victim's rights and assisted in forming the National Center for Missing and Exploited Children.

Mr. Walsh became host of the FOX-TV program, America's Most Wanted. On July 25th, 2006, President George W. Bush signed into law the Adam Walsh Child Protection and Safety Act. This act instituted a national database of convicted child molesters and sex offenders, and increased stiffer penalties for violence against children. In Adam's memory, a program is in place for lost children in department stores known as, Code Adam.

Adam Walsh

Chapter 36
Preface
Doctors Who Killed

Several doctors over the years have been Serial Killers including: Harold Shipman, Marcel Petiot, Michael Swango, H.H. Holmes, and John Bodkin Adams.

These are only some of the dozens who have been convicted. It is amazing that these people chose a profession to help save lives, but preferred to kill.

The Hippocratic Oath is pledged by every physician, swearing to practice medicine in an ethical manner. In my opinion, doctors that kill are actually 'Hypocrites,' which the dictionary defines as "a person who acts in contradiction to his or her stated beliefs or feelings." Is it not their job to curtail suffering and death? We sometimes put our lives in the hands of doctors, trusting that our best interests are the most important to them.

Thankfully, there are only a handful

of doctors who have been inclined to murder their patients, and they do not represent the millions of doctors who genuinely care and uphold their oaths.

Nevertheless, it's not only doctors who have killed in healthcare; there have been several nurses convicted for serial killing as well. Nurse Donald Harvey, for example, killed eight-seven patients and claimed that he started killing to "ease the pain" of patients, but eventually found it to be a sadistic pleasure. His methods included cyanide, arsenic, massive amounts of morphine, turning off ventilators, overdosing on insulin, adding tainted fluid to IVs gathered from patients with Hepatitis B or HIV, inserting a coat hanger into a catheter to cause kidney failure, and suffocation. Harvey is currently serving three life sentences.

Chapter 37

Name: Dr. Joseph Michael Swango
Born: October 21st, 1954
Place: Tacoma, Washington
Killing Span: 1981 – 1997
Number of Killings: 60
Captured: June, 1997

Michael Swango is a former licensed physician and an American serial killer. He was also known as Doctor of Death. While he was in medical school, Swango's classmates gave him the nickname

"Double-O-Swango" in reference to James Bond's 007 as any patient he met would apparently die soon thereafter.

Born in Washington but raised in Quincy, Illinois, he was the middle child of Muriel and John Swango. Michael's father was a United States Army Officer who served in the Vietnam War, and who later fell into alcoholism. Michael grew close to his mother as his father was away to war. Upon his return from Vietnam, John Swango became depressed and soon after his wife divorced him.

Michael Swango was an intelligent student in grade school. He spoke as class valedictorian in his senior year, played the clarinet, and was a member of the Quincy Notre Dame band. Post high school, he joined the U.S. Marine Corp but never saw any action, and was honorably discharged in 1976. While in the Marines, he took a great interest in physical fitness. After being discharged, he was often seen in the gym or jogging.

Swango enrolled at Quincy College, graduating *summa cum laude*. He was awarded the American Chemical Society

Award and moved on to medical school at Southern Illinois University School of Medicine. It was during his time at the university that he exhibited disconcerting behavior. Although he was a bright student, he was also known to be sluggish, preferring to work as an ambulance attendant rather than focus on his medical studies. It was also noted at this time that he had an attraction to dying patients. No one thought much of it at the time, but many patients to which Swango was assigned for routine checkups ended up "coding," and suffering life frightening emergencies; five of them passed away. Swango's halfhearted approach to his studies caught up with him only a month before he was due to graduate. It was exposed that he had forged patient checkups during his OB/GYN rotation. He was almost disqualified, but was allowed to remain when one member of the committee voted to give him a second chance. At the time, a unanimous vote was mandatory for a student to be dismissed.

However, even before that happened, several students and faculty members had raised alarm about Swango's capability to practice medicine. In the end, the school permitted him to graduate a year after his class with the stipulation that he repeat the OB/GYN rotation and complete several assignments in other specialties.

Although his dean gave him a very poor assessment, Swango still managed to get a surgical internship at Ohio State University Medical Center in 1983, and soon rose to a placement in neurosurgery. While he worked at the Rhodes Hall wing, nurses began observing that genuinely healthy patients began dying inexplicably with alarming regularity each time Dr. Swango was the intern on the floor. One nurse caught him injecting medicine (or not medicine) into a patient who later became peculiarly sick. The nurses reported their unease to administrators, but were accused of being paranoid. Swango was cleared by a quick investigation in 1984.

While at Ohio State University Medical Center, part of Swango's residency included a one-month rotation at

Columbus Children's Hospital. There were sufficient suspicions at this point that he was required to have someone else with him at all times while at the Children's Hospital. Nurses were instructed not to call him even if he was listed as the doctor on call, and he was not appointed to a position as physician once his internship ended in June of 1984.

In July of 1984, Swango went back to Quincy College and started working as an Emergency Medical Technician (EMT) with the Adams County Ambulance Corps even though he had been dismissed from another ambulance service for making a heart patient drive himself to the hospital. It did not take long for other paramedics on staff to begin noticing that every time Swango made the coffee or brought food, several of them would become brutally ill for no apparent reason. Just three months later, Swango was arrested by the Quincy Police Department and arsenic and other poisons were discovered in his custody. He was convicted on August 23rd, 1985, of aggravated battery for poisoning co-workers, and subsequently sentenced to five years in prison. Franklin County, Ohio prosecutors also considered charges of murder and attempted murder against Swango, but decided against it for lack of physical evidence.

In 1989, Swango was released from prison. He found work as a counselor at the Ohio State Career Development Center in Newport News, Virginia. He was forced out, however, after being caught working on a scrapbook of disasters on work time. He then landed a job as a laboratory technician for ATI Coal in Newport News, Virginia, now Vanguard Energy, a division of CITA Logistics. During his time there, several employees required medical attention, complaining of unrelenting and increasing stomach pains.

About the same time, the good doctor (or not) met Kristin Kinney, a nurse at Riverside Hospital. Swango and Kinney fell in love, and planned to marry and settle down. Swango was employed as a lab technician until 1991, when he quit his position to look for a new position as a doctor. After he quit his job, the FBI commenced an investigation, questioning employees on several occasions, though Swango wasn't aware of it at the time.

In the same year, Swango legally changed his name to Daniel J. Adams, and applied for a residency program at Ohio Valley Medical Center in Wheeling, West Virginia. He wasn't successful; however, in July of 1992 he began working at Sanford USD Medical Center in Sioux Falls. In both applications, he forged several legal documents, including an actuality sheet from the Illinois Department of Corrections that falsified his criminal record. The sheet he submitted declared that he had been convicted of a misdemeanor after he'd gotten into a struggle with a co-worker, receiving six months in prison rather five years for the felony charge of poisoning that he served.

This was a very significant omission on his part, knowing very well that most states won't award a medical license to a convicted felon as they consider a felony conviction to be confirmation of unprofessional behavior. He forged a 'Restoration of Civil Rights' letter from then Governor Gerald L. Baliles of Virginia, stating that Baliles had reinstated Swango's right to vote and serve on a jury – based on reports from friends and colleagues that Swango had committed no additional crimes after his misdemeanor, and that he was leading a commendable lifestyle.

Swango established a genuine position at Sanford, but in October made the blunder of attempting to join the American Medical Association (AMA). The AMA did a more methodical background check than the medical center and found out about the poisoning conviction. That Thanksgiving day, The Discovery Channel aired an episode of Justice Files that included a segment on Swango. In the course of the AMA report and phone calls from terrified colleagues, Sanford Medical Center fired Swango.

Author's Note: Would this stop Swango or whatever his name was? Not likely.

The AMA quickly lost track of Swango as he'd managed to find a job in the Psychiatric Residency Program at the Stony Brook School of Medicine. His first rotation was in the Internal Medicine Department at the Veteran Affairs Medical

Center in Northport, New York. Once again, his patients began dying for no reason, and four months later his wife, Kinney, committed suicide. Sharon Cooper, Kinney's mom, was dismayed to find out a person with Swango's history could be permitted to practice medicine. She contacted a friend of Kinney's who was a nurse at Sanford. The nurse advised Sanford's Dean, Robert Talley, about Swango's whereabouts. Talley then telephoned Jordan Cohen, the dean at Stony Brook. Under extreme questioning from Alan Miller, the head of Stony Brook's Psychiatry department, Swango admitted that he had lied about his poisoning conviction in Illinois, and he was fired on the spot. The ensuing public outcry resulted in Cohen and Miller being forced to quit as well before the year was out. Before he resigned, however, Cohen, with knowledge about the past mistakes of other medical facilities, sent a warning about Swango to all the one hundred and twenty-five medical schools, and the one thousand teaching hospitals across the U.S, successfully disenabling Swango from receiving a medical residency anywhere in the United States of America.

Since the incidents at the Veteran Affair's facility, federal authorities had gotten involved. Swango dropped out of sight until June of 1994, at which point the FBI discovered he was living in Atlanta, Georgia, working as a chemist at a computer equipment company's wastewater facility. The FBI notified the company and Swango was fired for lying on his job application. The FBI then obtained a warrant charging Swango with using falsified credentials to achieve entry to the Veteran Affair's Hospital.

By the time the warrant was executed, however, Swango had fled to Zimbabwe. There, he got a job at Mnene Lutheran Mission Hospital in the centre of the country, again based on phony documents, and again his patients began dying without explanation. As the Medical Director, Dr. Zishiri, had suspicions, Swango was suspended, but because the hospital was unable to complete satisfactory autopsies, no solid conclusions could be drawn to press charges. During his deferment, Swango hired a prominent lawyer by the name of David Coltart to facilitate him in returning to clinical practice. He also appealed to the authorities at Mpilo Hospital, Bulawayo, to permit him in the interim to continue working there voluntarily. This was opposed, however, by Dr. Abdollah Mesbah, a surgical resident, who had frequently found Swango snooping around on the wards and in ICU even when not on call. He'd suspected that some unexpected deaths could have been related to Swango, but he'd had no proof at that point.

Swango rented a room from a widow in Bulawayo who became ferociously sick after Swango prepared a meal for her and a friend. The woman consulted a local surgeon, Dr. Michael Cotton, who suspected arsenic poisoning and convinced her to send hair samples for forensic analysis to Pretoria. In due course, these clippings established toxic levels of arsenic in the hair. The lab reports were passed on by the Zimbabwe Central Intelligence Division, then through Interpol, and on to the FBI, who then visited Zimbabwe to interview Dr. Cotton, and the Pathologist in Bulawayo, Dr. Stanford Mathe.

Swango, however, had scented that the trap was about to be set and crossed the border into Zambia and then Namibia where he found temporary medical work. In March of 1997, he applied for a job at the Royal Hospital in Dhahran, Saudi Arabia, using a counterfeit résumé. While all this was taking place, Veteran Affair's Criminal Investigator Tom Valery consulted with Dr. Charlene Thomesen, a Forensic Psychiatrist, to help him with the case. She was able to analyze documents and data, and formulate a psychological profile of Dr. Swango, giving her evaluation of why he had committed such horrific crimes. Tom Valery was called by the FBI to discuss holding Swango. Valery then called Drug Enforcement Agency Agent Richard Thomesen who was stationed in the Manhattan DEA Office to discuss the investigation. Thomesen's conversation focused on Swango lying on his government application to work at the Department of Veterans Affairs, where he prescribed narcotic medications. This, and other proof, was sufficient for Immigration and Naturalization Service agents to arrest Swango in June of 1997 during a stopover at Chicago's O'Hare International Airport on his way to Saudi Arabia.

Faced with stiff evidence of his deceitful activities and the possibility of an extended inquest into his time in Zimbabwe, Swango pleaded guilty to defrauding the government in March of 1998 and in July was sentenced to three and a half years in prison. The sentencing judge ordered that Swango not be permitted to prepare or deliver food, or have any association with the preparation or distribution of drugs. He was charged with no counts of murder at this point, however. Not yet anyway. The FBI wanted to get their ducks in a row before charging him for his killings and needed hard evidence.

While Swango was serving his time, the fed's accumulated a substantial dossier of Swango's crimes. As part of that investigation, prosecutors obtained a warrant to exhume the bodies of three of his former patients and found poisonous chemicals in them. They also found indications that he had paralyzed Barron Harris, another patient, with an injection; Harris later lapsed into a coma and died. Furthermore, prosecutors found evidence that Swango had lied about the death of Cynthia Ann McGee, a patient to whom he had been attending while employed as an intern at OSU. Swango claimed she had suffered a heart blockage, but he had in fact killed her by injecting her with potassium that congested her heart. On July 11th, 2000, less than a week before he was scheduled to be released from prison on the fraud charge, Federal prosecutors on Long Island, New York, filed a criminal injustice charging Swango with three counts of murder, one count of assault, and one count each of false statements, mail deception, and conspiracy to commit wire fraud. At the same time, Zimbabwean authorities charged him with poisoning seven patients, five of whom had died.

Swango was officially indicted on July 17th, 2000, and insisted that he was not guilty. On September 6th, however, he capitulated and pled guilty of murder and fraud charges. Had he not done so, he faced the possibility of the death penalty and extradition to Zimbabwe. At his sentencing trial, prosecutors read shocking passages from Swango's notebook, describing the elation he felt during his crimes. Judge Mishler sentenced him to three consecutive life terms. He is currently incarcerated at The United States Penitentiary Administrative Maximum Facility (ADX) in Florence, Colorado. The FBI believes he may be responsible for as many as sixty deaths, which would make him one of the most inexhaustible serial killers in American history.

Chapter 38

Name: Dr. Marcel Petiot
Born: January 17th, 1897
Place: Auxerre, France
Killing Span: 1926 – 1944
Number of Killings: 60 plus
Captured: February, 1944

Marcel André Henri Félix Petiot is a former doctor and French Serial Killer. In 1944, he was convicted of numerous murders after the remains of twenty-six people were unearthed in his home in Paris. He is suspected, however, of killing about sixty people during his life, although the actual number remains unknown.

At seventeen, a psychiatrist diagnosed Petiot as mentally ill. As a boy, he was expelled from school many times. He did, however, finish his education in a special conservatory in Paris in July of 1915.

During World War I, Petiot volunteered for the French army and entered service in January of 1916. In the Second Battle of the Aisne, he was injured, gassed, and exhibited further symptoms of mental collapse. He was sent to various rest homes where he was arrested for stealing army blankets and eventually thrown into jail in Orléans, France. In a Psychiatric Hospital at Fleury-les-Aubrais, he was again diagnosed with assorted mental ailments, but was returned to the front in June of 1918, just before the war ended. He was transferred again only three weeks later after he shot himself in the foot, but attached to a new regiment in September. A new opinion of his mental condition was enough to get him discharged with a disability pension.

After the war ended, Petiot entered the accelerated education program proposed for war veterans. He completed medical school in eight months and became an intern at the Mental Hospital in Évreux. He received his Medical degree in December of 1921 and relocated to Villeneuve-sur-Yonne, where he received payment for his services from both his patients and government medical assistance funds. At this point, he was constantly abusing addictive narcotics, and acquired a reputation for questionable medical practices such as supplying narcotics, and performing illegal abortions.

Petiot's first victim is thought to have been Louise Delaveau, the daughter of an elderly patient, with whom he'd had an affair in 1926. Delaveau disappeared in May and neighbors later recalled that they had seen Petiot load a trunk into his car. Police investigated, but ultimately dismissed Delaveau as a runaway. That same year, Petiot ran for Mayor of the town, and hired an assistant to disrupt a political debate with his opponent. He won the election, and embezzled town funds while in office. In 1927, he married Georgette Lablais and together they had a son named Gerhardt.

The Prefect of Yonne Département received many complaints about Petiot's thefts and shady financial deals. Petiot was eventually suspended as Mayor in August of 1931 and subsequently resigned. He still had many supporters, however, and the village council resigned in commiseration. Five weeks later, on October 18th, he was elected as a councilor of Yonne Département. In 1932, he was accused of stealing electric power from the village and he lost his council seat.

Meanwhile, Petiot had already moved back to Paris. There, he attracted patients with made-up credentials, and built an impressive status for his practice. There were rumors, however, of unlawful abortions and unnecessary prescriptions for addictive remedies. In 1936, he was appointed médecin d'état-civil, with authority to write death certificates. That same year, he was briefly institutionalized for kleptomania, but released the following year.

When Germany defeated France in 1940, French citizens were drafted for forced labor in Germany. Petiot presented fake medical disability certificates to people who were drafted. He also treated the diseases of workers that had returned. In July of 1942, he was convicted of overprescribing narcotics, even though two addicts who would have testified against him had disappeared. He was fined 2400 French Francs for his crimes.

Petiot later claimed that throughout the period of German occupation he was engaged in confrontational activities. Allegedly, he developed covert weapons that killed Germans without leaving forensic evidence, planted booby traps all over Paris, had high-level meetings with Allied commanders, and worked with a fictional group of Spanish anti-fascists. However, there was no evidence to sustain any of these tall tales.

In 1980, however, he was cited by former United States Spymaster, Colonel John F. Grombach as a World War II resource. Grombach had been the founder and head of a small sovereign espionage agency, later known as The Pond, which operated from 1942 to 1955. Grombach declared that Petiot had reported the Katyn Forest massacre, German missile development at Peenemünde, and the names of Abwehr agents sent to the U.S. These claims were not maintained by any records of other intelligence services.

Petiot's most productive activity during the Occupation was his false escape method. Under the codename of Dr. Eugène, Petiot pretended to have a means of getting people wanted by the Germans, or the Vichy government, to safety outside France. He claimed that he could arrange a passageway to Argentina or elsewhere in South America through Portugal, for a price of 25,000 Francs per person. He had three accomplices to help with his scheme, Raoul Fourrier, Edmond Pintard, and René-Gustave Nézondet. They directed victims to Dr. Eugène, including Jews, Resistance fighters, and common criminals. Once the escapees were in his power, Petiot told them that Argentine officials required all entrants to the country to be vaccinated against diseases, and used this justification to inject them with cyanide. He then took all their valuables and disposed of their bodies.

At first, Petiot dumped the bodies in the Seine, but he later destroyed them by submerging them in quicklime or by incinerating them. In 1941, Petiot bought a house at 21 Rue le Sueur. What Petiot failed to do, however, was keep a low profile. The Gestapo eventually found out about him and, by April 1943, had heard all about this "route" for the escape of wanted people, which they assumed was part of the Resistance. Gestapo agent Robert Jodkum forced prisoner Yvan Dreyfus to approach the supposed network, but Dreyfus simply vanished. A later informer successfully infiltrated the operation, and the Gestapo arrested Fourrier, Pintard, and Nézondet. Under torture, they confessed that "Dr Eugène" was Marcel Petiot. Nezondet was later released but three others spent eight months in prison, suspected of helping Jews to escape. Even under suffering, they did not identify any other members of the Resistance. In reality, they knew of none.

The Gestapo released the three men in January of 1944. Two months later, Petiot's neighbors complained to police of a foul stink in the area, and about large amounts of smoke billowing from a chimney of a house in the neighborhood. Fearing a chimney fire, the police summoned firefighters who entered the house and discovered a roaring fire in a coal stove in the basement. In the fire, and scattered in the basement, were human remains. Petiot, however, was not there.

Over the next seven months, Petiot hid with friends, claiming the Gestapo wanted him for killing Germans and informers. He ultimately moved in with a patient, Georges Redouté, let his beard grow, and adopted various aliases.

During the deliverance of Paris in 1944, Petiot adopted the name "Henri Valeri" and connected with the French Forces of the Interior (FFI) in the uprising. He became a Captain in charge of counter-espionage and prisoner interrogations. When the newspaper, Resistance, published an article about Petiot, his defense attorney from the 1942 narcotics case received a letter in which his renegade client claimed the published allegations were lies. This gave police a hint that Petiot was still in Paris. The search began once more with "Henri Valeri" among those who were drafted to find him. Finally, on October 31st, 1944, Petiot was recognized at a Paris Métro station, and arrested. Among his possessions were a pistol, 31,700 Francs, and fifty sets of identity documents.

Petiot was imprisoned in La Santé Prison. He claimed that he was not guilty and that he had only killed enemies of France. He said that he had discovered the pile of bodies in February of 1944, but had assumed that they were associates killed by members of his Resistance network. The police, however, found that Petiot had no friends in any of the key Resistance groups. Some of the Resistance groups he spoke of had never existed, and there was no verification for any of his claimed exploits. Prosecutors finally charged him with at least twenty-seven murders for profit.

Their approximation of his ill-gotten gains was in excess of two hundred million Francs.

On March 19th, 1946, Petiot went on trial facing one hundred and thirty-five criminal charges. René Floriot acted for the defense against a panel consisting of state prosecutors and twelve civil lawyers hired by relatives of Petiot's victims. Petiot ridiculed the prosecuting lawyers, claiming that the assorted victims had all been collaborators or double agents, or that the vanished were living in South America under new names. He did finally admit to killing nineteen of the twenty-seven victims found in his house, claiming that they were Germans and collaborators, part of a total of sixty-three – what he called 'enemy kills.' His lawyer attempted to depict Petiot as a Resistance champion, but the judges and jurors were unimpressed. Petiot was convicted of twenty-six counts of murder and sentenced to death.

Petiot was beheaded on May 25th, 1946, after waiting a few days due to a problem in the release device of the guillotine.

Chapter 39

Name: Dr. Harold Frederick Shipman
Born: January 14th, 1946
Place: Nottingham, England
Killing Span: 1975–1998
Number of Killings: 218
Captured: September, 1998

Harold Frederick Shipman is a former doctor and a British Serial Killer. He is responsible for the deaths of 218 innocent patients.

Born in Nottingham, England, Shipman was the second of four children born to Harold and Vera Shipman. His working class parents were dedicated Methodists and Harold was very close to his mother who died of cancer when he was just seventeen. In the later stages of her disease, she had morphine administered at home by a doctor on June 21st, 1963.

Shipman was a bright student in school and he received a scholarship to attend Leeds School of Medicine, from which he graduated in 1970. After university, he started work at Pontefract General Infirmary in Pontefract, West Riding of Yorkshire, and in 1974, took his first position as a General Practitioner at the Abraham Ormerod Medical Centre in Todmorden, West Yorkshire. In 1975, he was caught forging prescriptions of Pethidine for his own personal use. He was fined £600, and temporarily attended a drug rehabilitation clinic in York. After a short stint as Medical Officer for Hatfield College, Durham, while doing temporary work for the National Coal Board, he became a General Practitioner at the Donneybrook Medical Centre in Hyde,

Greater Manchester, in 1977. Shipman continued working as a GP in Hyde throughout the 1980s and founded his own surgery practice on Market Street in 1993, becoming a beloved member of the community.

In March, 1998, Dr. Linda Reynolds of Brooke Surgery, in Hyde, encouraged by Deborah Massey from Frank Massey and Son's Funeral Parlor, expressed concerns to John Pollard, the Coroner for the South Manchester District, about the high death rate among Shipman's patients. In particular, she was troubled by the huge number of cremation forms for elderly women that he needed countersigned. The issue was brought to the attention of the police. The police, however, proved incapable of finding sufficient evidence to bring charges. The Shipman Inquiry afterward would blame the police for assigning inexperienced officers to the case. However, between April 17th, 1998, when the police discarded the investigation, and Shipman's ultimate arrest, he killed an additional three more people. His last victim was Kathleen

Grundy, a former Mayor of Hyde, who was found dead at her home on June 24th, 1998. Shipman was the last person to see her alive, and later signed her death certificate, recording 'old age' as cause of death.

Kathleen Grundy's daughter, Angela Woodruff, a lawyer, became concerned when Solicitor Brian Burgess informed her that a will had been produced, apparently by her mother, but that there were doubts about its authenticity. The will expelled Woodruff and her children, but left £386,000 to Dr. Shipman. Burgess told Woodruff to report it and went to the police, who then commenced an investigation. Grundy's body was exhumed, and when examined, found to contain traces of Diamorphine, also known as heroin, which is often used for controlling pain in terminal cancer patients. Shipman was arrested on September 7th, 1998, and was found to own a typewriter of the variety used to make the forged will.

The police then investigated other deaths Shipman had certified, and produced a list of fifteen sampling cases to investigate. They discovered a deadly pattern. Shipman would administer lethal overdoses of Diamorphine, sign patients' death certificates, and then forge medical records indicating that the patients had been in poor health.

On October 5th, 1999, Shipman's trial began. He was charged with the murders of Marie West, Ivy Lomas, Irene Turner, Lizzie Adams, Muriel Grimshaw, Jean Lilley, Marie Quinn, Bianka Pomfret, Kathleen Wagstaff, Norah Nuttall, Pamela Hillier, Maureen Ward, Joan Melia Winifred Mellor, and Kathleen Grundy, all of whom had died between 1995 and 1998.

After six days of deliberation, the jury found Shipman guilty of killing all fifteen of his patients by lethal injections of Diamorphine, and of forging the will of Kathleen Grundy. The trial judge sentenced him to fifteen successive life sentences and recommended that he never be released. Shipman also received four years for forging the will.

Shipman consistently denied his guilt, disputing the scientific facts against him. His defense tried and failed to have the count of murder of Mrs. Grundy, where a clear intention was alleged, tried separately from the others, where no noticeable motive was apparent. His wife, Primrose, denied his crimes as well. Although countless other cases could have been brought to court, the authorities concluded it would be hard to have a fair trial in view of the massive publicity surrounding the original trial. In addition, given the sentences from the first trial, an added trial was unnecessary. The Shipman Inquiry concluded that Shipman was probability responsible for about 218 deaths.

Shipman is the only doctor in British history to be found guilty of killing his patients.

According to historian Pamela Cullen, Dr. Adams had also been a serial killer, potentially killing up to 165 of his patients between 1946 and 1956, and it is projected he may have killed over 450 people, but as he was found not guilty, there was no movement to scrutinize the flaws in the system until the Shipman case. Had these matters been addressed earlier, it might have been more difficult for Shipman to commit his crimes.

In the early morning of January 13th, 2004, on the eve of his fifty-eighth birthday, a Prison Service statement from Wakefield Prison indicated that former doctor Shipman had hanged himself from the window bars of his cell using bed sheets. Some British tabloids articulated delight at his suicide and encouraged other serial killers to follow his example.

Some of the victims' families said they felt cheated as his suicide meant they would never have the satisfaction of Shipman's declaration of guilt, or answers as to why he committed his crimes. The Home Secretary, Mr. David Blunkett, noted that celebration was tempting, and said, "You wake up and you receive a call telling you Shipman has topped himself and you think, is it too early to open a bottle? And then you discover that everybody's very upset that he's done it."

Despite the Sun's celebration of Shipman's suicide, his death divided national newspapers, with the Daily Mirror branding him a "cold coward," and condemning the Prison Service for allowing his suicide to happen. The Independent, on the other hand, called for the inquiry into Shipman's suicide to look more widely at the state of Britain's prisons as well as the welfare of inmates. In The Guardian, an article by Sir David Ramsbotham (former Chief Inspector of Prisons) recommended that whole life sentences be replaced by imprecise sentences as these would give prisoners the hope of ultimate release, lessen the risk of their committing suicide, and potentially make the management of prisoners easier for prison officials.

Shipman's motive for suicide was never well known, but he had reportedly told his probation officer that he was considering suicide so his widow could receive a National Health Service (NHS) pension and lump sum, even though he had been stripped of his own pension. His wife received a full NHS pension, to which she would not have been entitled if he had died after the age of sixty.

Shipman had been encouraged to enroll in courses which would have coaxed him to confess his guilt. After refusing, he became emotional and close to tears when privileges, including the opportunity to telephone his wife, were revoked. These privileges had been returned the week before the suicide. Additionally, Primrose, who had consistently believed that Shipman was innocent, might have begun to suspect his guilt. According to Shipman's ex-cellmate, Tony Fleming, Primrose wrote her husband a letter exhorting him to "tell me everything, no matter what."

In January of 2001, Chris Gregg, a senior West Yorkshire detective, was chosen to direct an investigation into twenty-two of the West Yorkshire deaths. His report into Shipman's activities, submitted in July of 2002, concluded that Shipman had killed at least 215 of his patients between 1975 and 1998, during which time he practiced in Todmorden, West Yorkshire (1974–1975), and Hyde, Greater Manchester (1977–1998). Dame Janet Smith, the judge who tendered the report, admitted that several deaths that were more suspicious could not be definitively attributed to him. Most of his victims were elderly women in good health.

In her final report, issued January 24th, 2005, Judge Smith concluded the probable number of Shipman's victims between 1971 and 1998 to be approximately 250. However, in total, 459 people died while under his care, and it is unclear how many of those were Shipman's victims, as he was often the only doctor to certify a death.

The Shipman Inquiry also recommended changes to the structure of the General Medical Council. They charged six doctors who signed cremation forms for Shipman's victims with misconduct, claiming they should have noticed the connection between Shipman's home visits and his patients' deaths. Not all these doctors were found guilty, however. Shipman's widow, Primrose Shipman, was called to give verification about two of the deaths during the inquiry. She continued to maintain her husband's innocence both before and after the prosecution.

Chapter 40

Name: Dr. H. H. Holmes
Born: May 16th, 1861
Place: New Hampshire, USA
Killing Span: 1888–1894
Number of Killings: 27-200
Captured: November 17, 1894

Born Herman Webster Mudgett, but better known under the alias of Dr. Henry Howard Holmes, or Dr. H.H. Holmes. Holmes was a former doctor, and American Serial Killer.

Both Holmes' parents, Theodate

Page Price and Levi Horton Mudgett, came from the first non-native settlers in the area of New Hampshire. His father was a sadistic alcoholic and his mother a spiritual Methodist who read the Bible to Herman. When he was a youth, he claimed his schoolmates made him view and touch a human skeleton after they discovered he had a fear of the local doctor. Originally, the bullies brought him to the skeleton to frighten him, but Holmes was instead completely captivated by it, and soon became fanatically interested by death.

Holmes married Clara Lovering of Alton, New Hampshire on July 4th, 1878, and had a son with her named Robert on February 3rd, 1880. Holmes graduated from the University of Michigan Medical School in June of 1884 after passing all his tests and requirements. While he was enrolled in University, he would steal bodies from the laboratory, disfigure them, and claim that the people were killed accidentally, in order to collect insurance money from policies he took out on each of the deceased.

After university, Holmes relocated to

Chicago to pursue a career in Pharmaceuticals. While there, he also engaged in many unethical business, real estate, and promotional deals, under the name of H.H. Holmes.

Holmes lived in Chicago, but his wife and son still lived back in New Hampshire. While he was still married, Holmes met and married Myrta Belknap in Chicago on January 28th, 1887, and had a daughter, Lucy, in July of 1889. He lived with Myrta and Lucy in Wilmette, Illinois, and spent most of his time in Chicago tending to business. He filed for divorce from Clara after marrying Myrta, but the divorce was never finalized.

In January of 1894, Holmes also married Georgiana Yoke in Denver, Colorado, while still married to Myrta and Clara. Moreover, while married to the three of them, he also had an affair with Julia Smythe, the wife of one of his previous employees. She would later become one of Holmes' victims. To make a count, Holmes, at that point, had three wives and one girlfriend.

In the summer of 1886, Holmes came across Dr. E. S. Holton's Drugstore at the corner of S. Wallace and W. 63rd Street, in the neighborhood of Englewood. Dr. Holton's wife took care of the store while he was ailing from cancer. Weighed down by personal distress and the responsibility of managing a business, Mrs. Holton gave Holmes a job. Holmes proved himself an astute employee and when Dr. Holton passed away, Holmes used his well-honed charisma to console the grieving widow. Consequently, he convinced Mrs. Holton that selling the drugstore to him would alleviate the burden of her responsibilities. Holmes' proposal seemed like a godsend to the elderly woman and she agreed. Holmes purchased the store from her primarily with funds acquired by mortgaging the store's fixtures and inventory, the loan to be repaid in generous monthly installments of one hundred dollars, which would equate to about $3000.00 per month today.

However, Mrs. Holton disappeared mysteriously not long after Dr. Holton died. Holmes told people she was visiting relatives out in California. As people began asking after her return, he told them that she was enjoying California so much that she had decided to live there.

Dr. Holmes procured a parcel of land across from the drugstore where he built a three-story, block-long building that the neighborhood referred to as the Castle. It was opened as a hotel for the World's Columbian Exposition in 1893. Part of the formation was used as commercial space while the ground floor contained Holmes's own relocated Drugstore, as well as assorted shops. The upper two floors contained his personal office and over 100 windowless rooms with doorways opening onto to brick walls, abnormally angled hallways, stairways to nowhere, doors only operable from the outside, and a multitude of other bizarre and convoluted designs.

Holmes frequently altered the plans during the construction phase of the Castle so that only he fully understood the layout of the building. Thus, the possibility of being reported to the police as suspicious was lessened.

After the completion of the hotel,

Holmes required women who wanted to work for him to take out life insurance policies as a stipulation of being hired. Holmes would pay the premiums, but would also be the beneficiary. He tortured and killed some of his victims; others, he locked some in a soundproof bedroom fitted with gas lines that let him asphyxiate them at anytime; and some were locked in a huge soundproof bank vault near his office where they were left to suffocate.

The victims' bodies were dropped down a secret chute to the basement where many were carefully dissected, stripped of their flesh, crafted into skeleton models, and sold to medical schools. Holmes cremated the bodies, or placed them in lime pits for obliteration. He had two massive furnaces, pits of acid, bottles of assorted poisons, and even a stretching rack. Through the many connections he had gained in medical school, he sold the skeletons and organs of his victims with little difficulty.

Subsequent to the World's Fair in 1893, with creditors closing in and the economy in a general slump, Holmes skipped out of Chicago to avoid his debt. He reemerged in Fort Worth, Texas, where he had inherited property from two railroad heiress sisters. He promised to marry one of them, and then murdered them both. While in Texas, Holmes sought to construct another Castle along the same lines of his Chicago business. He soon abandoned this venture, however, finding the law enforcement climate in Texas unwelcoming.

Holmes continued to travel about the United States and Canada, and while it seems probable that he continued to kill, the only murders around him that can be confirmed during this period are those of his longtime associate, Benjamin Pitezel, and three of Pitezel's children, Alice, Nellie, and Howard.

In July of 1894, Holmes was detained and temporarily incarcerated for the first time for a charge related to horse fraud in St. Louis. He was swiftly bailed out; however, while in jail, he spoke with convicted train robber, Marion Hedgepeth who was serving a twenty-five year sentence. Holmes had invented a plan to deceive an insurance company out of $10,000 by taking out a policy on himself and then faking his own death. Holmes promised to pay Hedgepeth a $500.00 fee in exchange for the name of a lawyer who could be trusted. He was directed to Colonel Jeptha Howe, the brother of a public defender, who commended Holmes's scheme. Holmes's plan to sham his own death failed, however, when the insurance company became apprehensive and refused to pay. Holmes did not press his claim. He instead concocted a comparable plan with his associate, Benjamin Pitezel, a carpenter with a criminal past who Holmes met during construction of the Castle in 1889.

Pitezel had arranged to fake his own death so that his wife could collect on the $10,000 policy which she was to divide with Holmes and the shady attorney, Howe. The scheme was to take place in Philadelphia. Pitezel would set himself up as an inventor under the name B. F. Perry, and then be killed and disfigured in a lab explosion. Holmes was to find a suitable corpse to play the role of Pitezel. Of course, Holmes killed Pitezel instead. Forensic evidence offered at Holmes's later trial indicated that chloroform was used in Pitezel's death, seemingly to fake suicide (Pitezel had been an alcoholic and chronic depressive). Using Pitezel's genuine corpse, Holmes collected on the insurance policy. He then coerced Pitezel's wife into allowing three of her five children Nellie, Alice, and Howard, to stay in his custody. The eldest daughter and baby remained with Mrs. Pitezel.

Holmes travelled with the children through the northern United States and into Canada – Mrs. Pitezal travelled along an alternate route – all the while using a mixture of aliases and lying to Mrs. Pitezel concerning her husband's death, claiming that Pitezel was in hiding in South America. A Philadelphia detective by the name of Frank Geyer tracked Holmes, and found the decomposed bodies of two of the Pitezel girls in Toronto, Canada. He then followed Holmes to Indianapolis where Holmes had rented a cottage and was reported to have visited a local pharmacy to purchase drugs to kill young Howard

Pitezel, and a repair shop to sharpen the knives he used to dismember the boy's body before he burned it. The boy's teeth and bits of bone were later discovered in the home's chimney. In 1894, Marion Hedgepeth, Holmes's former jail mate, tipped off the police because Holmes had neglected to pay him off as promised for his help.

On November 17th, 1894, Dr. H.H. Holmes's murder spree finally ended when he was arrested in Boston after being tracked there from Philadelphia by the Pinkertons. He was held on an outstanding warrant for horse theft in Texas, as the authorities had little more than reservations at this point, and Holmes appeared on the brink of fleeing the country in the company of his unsuspecting third wife.

After the caretaker for the Castle informed police that he was never permitted to clean the upper floors, police began a meticulous investigation. Over the course of the next month, Holmes's resourceful methods of committing murders and then disposing of the corpses were revealed. A mysterious fire consumed the building on August 19th, 1895. The site is now occupied as a U.S. Post Office.

As Holmes remained in prison in Philadelphia, police in both Chicago and Philadelphia police started an investigation into his operations; in particular, into the whereabouts of the three missing children, with Philadelphia detective Frank Geyer given the undertaking of finding answers. His pursue of the children, like the search of Holmes's Castle, received extensive publicity. His eventual discovery of their remains fundamentally sealed Holmes's destiny, at least in the public mind. Holmes was put on trial for the murder of Pitezel. Holmes confessed to the murder, and after his conviction, thirty more murders in Chicago, Indianapolis and Toronto, and six attempted murders, were added to his charge.

Holmes was paid $7500.00 by Hearst Newspapers in exchange for his story. He gave various ambiguous accounts, claiming initially that he was pure, later claiming that he was possessed by Satan. His talent for lying has made it complicated for researchers to ascertain any legitimacy in his statements.

On May 7th, 1896, Holmes was hanged at the Philadelphia County Prison. Until the time of his death, he remained quiet and cordial, showing very few signs of fear, anxiety, or depression. Holmes's neck did not snap immediately. He died slowly, twitching over fifteen minutes before being pronounced dead twenty minutes after the trap had been sprung.

Chapter 41

Name: Dr. John Bodkin Adams
Born: January 21st, 1899
Place: Randalstown, County Antrim, Ireland
Killing Span: 1946 - 1956
Number of Killings: 160
Captured: December, 1956

John Bodkin Adams was born just before the turn of the century to a profoundly religious family of Plymouth Brethren of which he remained a member for his whole life. His father, Samuel, was a preacher in the local congregation, though by profession he was a watchmaker. John had a brother, William, who was born in 1903, but died at the age of fifteen from the 1918 influenza pandemic.

Adams graduated in 1921 from Queen's University in Belfast, although he missed a year of studies due to tuberculosis. His professors thought him a plodder and distant from his fellow schoolmates. From university he was hired straight away by Dr. Arthur Short as an assistant in the British Royal Infirmary. After spending a year there, however, it did not work out for him and he applied for a General Practitioner's position in a Christian practice in Eastbourne, where he worked for many years while living with his cousin and his mother. In 1929, he borrowed £2000 from a rich patient, William Mawhood, and purchased an eighteen-room house in Trinity Trees called Kent Lodge.

Adams would regularly invite himself to the Mawhoods' house at mealtime, even bringing his mother and cousin. He also began charging items to their accounts at local stores without their consent. Mrs.

Mawhood would later portray Adams to the police as "a real scrounger." When Mr. Mawhood died in 1949, Adams visited his widow uninvited, and took a 22-carat gold pen from her bedroom dressing table, saying he wanted "something of her husband's." After that he never visited her again.

Rumor regarding Adams's eccentric methods had started by the mid 1930s. In 1935, Adams inherited £7,385 from a patient, Matilda Whitton. Her will was contested by her relatives, but the court upheld it; a supplement giving Adams's mother £100 was reversed, however. Adams then began receiving anonymous postcards about how he was "bumping off" patients, as he told a newspaper interviewer in 1957. These were received at a rate of three or four per year until the war; they then commenced again in 1945.

Adams stayed in Eastbourne throughout the war, infuriated at not being sought-after by other doctors to be selected for a "pool system" where General Practitioners would treat the patients of colleagues who had been drafted. In 1941, he achieved a diploma in Anesthetics and worked in a local hospital one day a week where he earned a reputation as a bungler. He would fall asleep during operations, count his money, eat cakes, and even mix up the anesthetic gas tubes, leading to patients waking up or turning blue. His mother died in 1943, and in 1952 his cousin Sarah developed cancer. Adams gave her an injection half an hour before she died.

By 1956, John Adams was one of the wealthiest doctors in England, having enjoyed a successful career. Despite rumors about his ethics and fraudulent wills, he was seen with some of the most influential people in the country, including Members of Parliament, Sir Alexander Maguire, the 10th Duke of Devonshire, Chief of Police Richard Walker, famous painter Oswald Birley, and a host of powerful business people.

On July 23rd, 1956, the Eastbourne Police received an unidentified call about a death. It was from Leslie Henson, the music hall performer, whose friend Gertrude Hullett had died suddenly while being treated by Dr. Adams.

The investigation was turned over from Eastbourne Police on August 17th to two officers from the Metropolitan Police's Murder Squad. The senior officer was Detective Superintendent Herbert Hannam of Scotland Yard, noted for having solved the infamous Teddington Towpath Murders in 1953. He was assisted by a junior Officer, Detective Sergeant Charles Hewett. The investigators decided to focus on cases from 1946 to 1956 only. Of the three hundred and ten death certificates examined by Home Office Pathologist, Francis Camps, one hundred and sixty-three were believed to be of suspicious nature. Apparently, many patients had been given "special injections" of substances that Dr. Adams refused to explain to the nurses caring for his patients.

Furthermore, it became known that his routine was to ask the nurses to leave the room before injections were given. He would also segregate patients from their relatives, hindering contact between them. On August 24th, in an astonishing move, the

British Medical Association (BMA) sent a letter to all Doctors in Eastbourne, reminding them of Professional Secrecy – like patient confidentiality, for example – if interviewed by the police. It was obvious the BMA was trying to cover their asses in the event of lawsuits. Lead Detective Hannam was not impressed, especially since any information gleaned would relate to dead patients. He, and the Attorney General, Sir Reginald Manningham-Buller, who prosecuted all cases of poisoning, wrote to the BMA secretary, Dr. Macrae, "to try to get him to remove the ban." The gridlock continued until November 8th when Sir Reginald Manningham-Buller met with Dr. Macrae to persuade him of the significance of the case. During this meeting, in a highly extraordinary move, he passed Hannam's confidential one hundred and eight-seven page report on Dr. Adams over to Dr Macrae. Dr Macrae then took the report to the President of the BMA and returned it the next day.

In all likelihood, Macrae photocopied the report and passed it on to the defense lawyers. Certain of the seriousness of the accusations, Dr. Macrae dropped his resistance to doctors talking to the police. In the end though, only two Eastbourne doctors ever submitted evidence.

On 24th November, Detectives Hannam, Hewett, and the head of Eastbourne Central Intelligence Division, Detective Inspector Pugh, presented Dr. Adams with a search warrant under the Dangerous Drugs Act of 1951. When the detectives told him that they were looking for morphine, heroin, Pethidine, and the like, Adams was surprised and said, "Oh, that group. You will find none here. I have not any. I very seldom ever use them." Then Detective Hannam asked for Adams' Dangerous Drugs Register, the record of those ordered and used, and Adams replied, "I don't know what you mean. I keep no register." In fact, he hadn't kept one since 1949. When they showed him a list of dangerous drugs that he had prescribed Morrell, and asked who had administered them, Adams replied, "I did nearly all; perhaps the nurses gave some but mostly me." This contradicted what the nurses' notebooks would show during his trial. Detective Hannam then said, "Doctor, you prescribed for her seventy-five 1/6th grains of heroin tablets the day before she died," to which Dr. Adams replied, "Poor soul, she was in terrible agony. It was all used. I used them myself. Do you think it is too much?"

As the investigators inspected Adams's cupboards, he walked to another and slipped two objects into his jacket pocket. Hannam and Pugh saw this occur and challenged Adams. He then showed them two bottles of morphine, one of which he said was for Annie Sharpe, a patient and major witness who had died nine days earlier under his care; the other he said was for Mr. Soden, who happened to die on September 17th, 1956, but pharmacy records later showed that Mr. Soden had never been prescribed morphine. After his main trial, Adams would also be charged and convicted with obstructing the lawful search, concealing the bottles, and for failing to keep a dangerous drugs register. Later at the police station, Adams told Hannam, "Easing the passing of a dying person isn't all that wicked. Mrs. Morrell wanted to die. That can't be murder. It is impossible to accuse a doctor." In the basement of Adams's house, police found a lot of unused china and silverware. In one room, there were twenty new car tires still in their wrappings and several other car parts. Wines and spirits were stored in quantity. On the second floor, one room was devoted solely for weapons; there were six guns in a glass display case, and several automatic pistols, though he had permits for these. Another room was used completely for photographic equipment. Left lying around were a dozen very expensive cameras in leather cases.

In December, the police obtained a memorandum belonging to a Daily Mail journalist pertaining to rumors of homosexuality between a police officer, a magistrate, and a doctor. The letter directly implicated Dr. Adams. This information had come, according to the reporter, directly from Detective Hannam. The magistrate was Sir Roland Gwynne, Mayor of Eastbourne from 1929 to 1931 and brother of Rupert Gwynne, Member of Parliament for Eastbourne from 1910 to 1924. Sir Gwynne was Adams' patient and it was well known that he would visit Adams every day at 9 a.m. The pair went on numerous holidays together and had just spent three weeks in Scotland that September. The officer in question was the Deputy Chief Constable of Eastbourne, officer Alexander Seekings. Detective Hannam ignored this line of inquest, however (even though homosexual acts were an offence in 1956), and the police, as an alternative, gave the journalist a reprimand. The memo, though, was verification of Adams' close connections to those of power in Eastbourne at the time.

On December 19th, 1956, Dr. Adams was arrested at Kent Lodge. As he was walking out with the police, he told his secretary, "I will see you in heaven."

The investigators had only collected enough evidence to charge Adams with one murder thus far, the murder of Edith Morrell. They were still trying to tie together the Clara Miller, Gertrude Hullett, Dr. Hullett, and Julia Bradnum murders.

Adams was first tried for the murder

of Mrs. Morrell, with the Hullett charge to be prosecuted afterwards. The trial lasted seventeen days, the longest murder trial in Britain up to that point. It was presided over by 'Mr. Justice,' Patrick Devlin. Devlin summed up the delicate nature of the case: "It is a most curious situation, perhaps unique in these courts that the act of murder has to be proved by expert evidence." Defense Counsel, Sir Frederick Geoffrey Lawrence, a specialist in real estate and divorce cases, a relative stranger in a criminal court and defending his first murder trial, told the jury that there was no evidence that a murder had been committed, much less that a murder had been committed by Dr. Adams.

He emphasized that the indictment was based primarily on testimonies from the nurses who tended to Morrell and that none of the witnesses' evidence coordinated with the others. On the second day of the trial, he produced notebooks written by the nurses, detailing Adams' treatment of Morrell. The prosecution claimed never to have seen these notebooks, even though they were recorded in pretrial lists of evidence. These differed from the nurses' recollection of events, and showed that smaller quantities of drugs were given to the patient than the prosecution had thought, based on Adams' prescriptions.

Furthermore, the prosecution's two expert medical witnesses gave contradictory opinions. Dr. Arthur Douthwaite was prepared to say that murder had definitely been committed, but he changed his mind in the middle of his testimony regarding the exact date. Dr. Michael Ashby was more uncommunicative. Defense witness, Dr. John Harman, however, was adamant that Adams' treatment, though atypical, was not irresponsible. Finally, the prosecution was surprised that the defense did not call upon the long-winded Adams himself to give evidence, and thereby chat himself to the gallows. This was much unanticipated, shocking the prosecution and the press, and even surprised the judge.

When the jury retired to converse about the verdict, Lord Chief Justice Rayner Goddard phoned Devlin to urge him, if

Adams were found not guilty, to grant Adams bail before he was to be tried on a second count of murdering Gertrude Hullett. Devlin was taken aback at this since a person accused of murder had never been given bail before in English legal history. During the committal hearing prior to the trial, Chief Justice Goddard had been seen dining with Sir Roland Gwynne at the White Hart hotel in Lewes. Goddard, as Lord Chief Justice, had by then already appointed Devlin to try Adams' case.

On April 9th, 1957, after just forty-four minutes of deliberating, the jury returned their verdict of not guilty. The public was blown away. Even those in the law community were astonished as the evidence against Adams was over-whelming. It was generally agreed that money speaks louder than murder.

It is worth mentioning that some of the evidence gathered by Detective Hannam during the investigation was never permitted to be aired in court. Taken together, they suggest a certain modus operandi. The jury did not hear the following:

August of 1939 – Adams was treating Agnes Pike. Her solicitors, however, were concerned about the amount of hypnotic drugs he was giving her and asked another doctor, Dr. Mathew, to take over treatment. Dr. Mathew examined Pike in Adams's presence, but could find no disease present. Furthermore, the patient was deeply under the influence of drugs, incoherent, and gave her age as 200 years old. Later, during the examination, Adams stepped forward unexpectedly and gave Pike an injection of morphine. When asked why he did this, Adams replied, "Because she might be violent." Dr. Mathew discovered that Adams had banned all relatives from seeing her, and withdrew Adams' medication. After eight weeks of his care, Agnes Pike was able to do her own shopping and had regained her full faculties.

December of 1946 – Emily Louise Mortimer died at age seventy-five. Afterwards, Adams took a bottle of brandy and a clock from her room. He claimed the clock had been loaned by him and that it was not "right to leave spirits in a nursing home." Adams received the remainder from Mortimer's will and by 1957 had earned £1,950 in dividends from the shares he inherited.

February 23rd, 1950 – Amy Ware died at the age of seventy-six. Dr. Adams had prohibited her from seeing relatives prior to her death. She left Adams £1000 of her total estate of £8,993, yet Adams stated on the cremation form that he was not a beneficiary of the will. He was charged and convicted for this in 1957.

December 28th, 1950 – Annabelle Kilgour died at age eighty-nine. She had been attended by Adams since July when she had a stroke. She went into a coma on December 23rd, immediately after Adams started giving her sedatives. The nurse involved later told the police that she was very certain Adams either gave her the wrong injection or far too concentrated a type. Mrs. Kilgour left Adams £200 and a clock.

January 3rd, 1952 – Adams purchased 5,000 Phenobarbitone tablets. By the time his house was searched four years later, none were left.

May 11th, 1952 – Julia Bradnum died at the age of eighty-five. The previous year, Adams asked her if her will was in order, and accompanied her to the bank to check. On examining it, he pointed out that she had not given her beneficiaries addresses and that it should be rewritten. She had wanted to leave her house to her adopted daughter, but Adams suggested it would be best to sell the house and then give money to whomever she wanted, and that is what she did. Adams ultimately received £661. While Adams attended Bradnum, he was frequently seen holding her hand and chatting to her on one knee. The day before Mrs. Bradnum died, she had been doing housework and going for walks. The next morning she woke up feeling sick. Adams was called. He gave her an injection and stated, "It will be over in three minutes." It was. Adams then confirmed, "I'm afraid she's gone," and left the room.

Mrs. Bradnum was exhumed on December 21st, 1956. Adams had written on the death certificate that she had died of a cerebral hemorrhage. Dr. Francis Camps examined her brain, however, and excluded this likelihood. The rest of the body, unfortunately, was not in good enough condition to ascertain the real cause of death. Furthermore, it was noticed that Adams, the executor, had put a plate on Bradnum's coffin stating that she had died on May 27th, 1952. This was the date her body was interred.

November 22nd, 1952 – Julia Thomas, seventy-two, was being treated by Adams (she called him "Bobbums") for depression after her cat died in early November. On the 19th, Adams gave her sedatives so she would feel "better for it in the morning." The next day, after more tablets, she went into a coma. On the 21st he told Thomas' cook, "Mrs. Thomas has promised me her typewriter, I'll take it now." She died at 3 am the next morning.

January 15th, 1953 – Hilda Neil Miller, eighty-six, died in a guesthouse where she lived with her sister, Clara. They had not been receiving their mail for several months previously, and were cut off from their relatives. When Hilda's long-standing friend, Dolly Wallis, asked Adams about her health, he answered her with medical terms she "did not understand." While visiting Hilda, Adams was seen by her nurse, Phyllis Owen, to pick up articles in the room, examine them, and slip them in his pocket. Adams arranged Hilda's funeral and burial site himself.

February 22nd, 1954 – Clara Neil Miller died at age eighty-seven. Adams often locked the door when he saw her for up to twenty minutes at a time. When Dolly Wallis asked about this, Clara said he was assisting her in "personal matters" – pinning on brooches, adjusting her dress. His fat hands were "comforting" to her. She also appeared to be under the control of drugs. Early that February, the coldest for many years, Adams had sat with her in her room for forty minutes. A nurse entered unnoticed and saw Clara's "bed clothes all off and over the foot rail of the bed, her night gown up around her chest, and the window in the room open top and bottom while Adams read to her from the Bible. When later confronted by Detective Hannam regarding this, Adams said, "The person who told you that doesn't know why I did it."

Clara willed Adams £1,275 and he charged her estate a further £700 after her death. He was the sole executor of her will. Her funeral was arranged by Adams and only he and Annie Sharpe, the guesthouse owner, were present. She received £200 in Clara's will; Adams tipped the minister a guinea after the ceremony. Clara was one of the two bodies exhumed during the police investigation on December 21st, 1956. Dr. Francis Camps concluded that she had suffered from bronchopneumonia, probably brought about by high drug doses, not a heart problem, as Adams had said on the death certificate. According to prescription records, Adams had not prescribed anything to treat the bronchopneumonia.

May 30th, 1955 – James Downs, brother-in-law of Amy Ware (see above), died at the age of eighty-eight. He had entered a nursing home with a broken ankle four months earlier. Adams treated him with a sedative containing morphine which made him absentminded. On April 7th, Adams gave his nurse, Sister Miller, a tablet to give to Downs to make him more alert. Two hours later, a solicitor arrived for Downs to amend his will. Adams told the solicitor that he was to be made a beneficiary to inherit £1000. The solicitor amended the will and returned two hours later with another doctor, Dr. Barkworth, who confirmed the patient to be alert. Dr. Barkworth was paid three guineas for his time. Nurse Miller later told police that she had heard Adams earlier in April tell the "senile" Mr. Downs, "Now look Jimmy, you promised me you would look after me and I see you haven't even mentioned me in your will. I have never charged you a fee." Downs died after a thirty-six-hour coma, twelve hours after Adams's last visit. Adams charged his estate £216 for his services and signed Downs' cremation form, stating he had "no financial interest in the death of the deceased."

March 14th, 1956 – Dr. Alfred John Hullett died at only seventy-one. He was the husband of Gertrude Hullett. Shortly after his death, Adams went to a Chemist to get a 10cc hypodermic morphine solution in the name of Mr. Hullett containing five grains of morphine, asking for the prescription to be backdated to the previous day. The police alleged this was to cover morphine Adams had given him from his own private supplies. Dr. Hullett also left Adams £500 in his will.

November 15th, 1956 – Annie Sharpe, owner of the guesthouse where the Neil Millers' had died, and consequently a major witness, died suddenly of carcinomatosis of the peritoneal cavity while detectives Hannam and Hewett were in London conducting their investigation. Adams had diagnosed her with cancer just five days earlier, and had given her a prescription for hypodermic morphine and thirty-six Pethidine tablets. The police were very frustrated. They'd had two chances to interview Sharpe, and Hannam and Hewett felt she had been about to reveal information. She was cremated quickly, precluding an investigation into her death. Detective Hannam also revealed that four members of Adams' household staff had been given morphine, heroin, or Pethidine by Adams in prescription form. Adams obtained these on the National Health

Service, leading the detectives to conclude that he was merely using their names and keeping the drugs for his own supplies an act of fraud.

In the aftermath of the trial, Adams resigned from the National Health Service and was convicted in Lewes Crown Court on July 26th, 1957, on eight counts of forging prescriptions, four counts of making false statements on cremation forms, and three offences under the Dangerous Drugs Act of 1951; he was fined £2,400 plus costs of £457. His license to prescribe dangerous drugs was revoked on September 4th and on November 27th he was removed from the Medical Register by the GMC. Adams continued to see some of his more steadfast patients, prescribing over the counter medicine to them.

Preceding the trial, Percy Hoskins, chief crime reporter for the Daily Express, whisked Adams off to a safe house where he spent the next two weeks relating his life story. Hoskins had befriended Adams during the trial and was the only major journalist to disbelief his guilt. Adams was paid £10,000 for the interview, though he never spent the proceeds; the money was found in a bank vault after his death. Adams then successfully sued several newspapers for libel. He returned to Eastbourne where he continued to practice privately regardless of the common belief in the town that he had murdered people. This belief was not shared by his friends and patients in general. One exception was Roland Gwynne, who distanced himself considerably from Adams after the trial.

Dr. Adams was given back his license as a General Practitioner on November 22nd, 1961, after two failed applications; his ability to prescribe dangerous drugs was restored the following July. In August of 1962, Adams applied for a visa to America but was refused because of his dangerous drug convictions.

Adams slipped and fractured his hip on June 30th, 1983 while shooting in Battle, East Sussex. He was taken to Eastbourne hospital but developed a chest infection and died on July 4th of left ventricular failure.

Chapter 42
Preface
Unsolved Serial Murder Cases

It is very frightening when serial murders are happening in a community. Just knowing there is someone stalking the neighborhood, looking for victims, is very frightening. Many of these killers hunt in the same area for years; others travel around spreading their fear in new regions and, luckily, many of them are captured. When the killer is not captured, however, the public is forced to envision when he or she will strike again.

There is sorrow in knowing that a serial killer was never brought to justice for the crimes they committed. There are several unsolved murder cases in the United States alone, not counting all around the globe, that are thought to have been the work of a serial killer. The following are short stories of unsolved cases.

Chapter 43
The Zodiac Killer
San Francisco, California
(39+ Victims)

The identity of the Zodiac killer is unknown and probably will always be, but FBI has not stopped looking, and updates are made to the file regularly. In the 1960s and 1970s, the serial killer operated in the North of California. Normally, the media or police dub a serial killer. This arrogant killer, however, made up his own, calling himself Zodiac in a series of letters he sent to the media.

The Zodiac claims, by way of letters, to have killed thirty-seven people. Authorities only know of seven confirmed victims. It all started on December 20th, 1968, when David Faraday and Betty Lou Jensen were on their first date together, and planned to go to a Christmas concert, but first drove out to Lake Herman Road, which was a "lover's lane." About a half hour later, their bodies were discovered, and the Sheriff's office was notified. Both had been shot dead.

Darlene Ferrin and Michael Mageau went for a drive on July 4th, 1969 and parked just four miles from the first murder site. Another car drove up and immediately drove away. Ten minutes later, the car returned and parked behind them. The killer shot both of them with a 9mm Luger, firing seven shots. Darlene Ferrin was shot in the chest, neck, and face. The Vallejo Police received a call from a man the next day reporting himself to be the killer, claiming he killed the couple back in December. The police traced the call to a phone booth, but no evidence was left, and police had no suspect.

The Vallejo Times Herald, the San Francisco Chronicle, and the San Francisco Examiner, each received a letter on August 1st, 1969, supposedly from the killer, taking credit for the murders. The catch was that each newspaper only received 1/3rd each of the 408 symbol cryptic letter that the killer claimed would identify him. He demanded the letters be printed on the front pages of their papers or he would kill a dozen people over the weekend. This turned out to be a bluff as the Chief of Police Jack Stiltz said in the Chronicle *"We're not satisfied that the letter was written by the murderer."* The Chronicle, however, did publish their part on page four, but no murder took place over the weekend. The other newspapers also published their pieces, but not on the front page, and not the next day. The cryptic code was cracked by civilians, Bettye and Donald Harden, of Salinas, California, on August 8th, 1969. What it contained was not the identity of the killer, as the killer had claimed, but a message claiming the killer was collecting slaves for the afterlife.

Cecelia Shepard and Bryan Hartnell were college students at Pacific Union and on September 27th, 1969, they were having a picnic at Lake Berryessa when a man approached them wearing a hoodie and sunglasses. On his chest hung a 3"x3" circular cross-like symbol. He had a gun but never used it. Instead, he tied both of them up and stabbed them. He proceeded to draw a circular cross symbol on Bryan's car with a pen, and then wrote beneath it, *"Vallejo/12-20-68/7-4-69/Sept   27-69-6:30/by knife."* The killer then made a call to the Sheriff's office from a payphone to report the crime. The police got a wet print off the phone, but it did not match any criminal in their system.

Cecelia Shepard went into a coma and passed away two days later. Bryan Hartnell, however, survived, and gave a good recount to the police and media about what happened, and what the perp looked like.

It's interesting to make a note that

Detective Ken Narlow of the Napa County Sheriff's office was assigned to the investigation at the start, and continued working the case until his retirement in 1987, and even then, investigated on his own until he passed away at eighty years old on December 2nd, 2010. Talk about dedication.

In San Francisco on October 11th, 1969, a cab driver by the name of Paul Stine stopped for a passenger when he was instantly shot in the head with a 9mm gun. Three teenagers witnessed the killer take the cabbie's money, tear off a piece of the driver's shirt, and wipe down the cab. They each gave a description of the killer and more composite sketches were drawn up. Over the years following, detectives investigated over 2500 suspects under the tutelage of Detectives Dave Toschi and Bill Armstrong. The killings were all happening in Northern California; thus each county would have to investigate the murders in their own backyards.

The Zodiac killer prepared another letter and just three days later on October 14th, the Chronicle received it along with a swatch of the cab driver's shirttail to prove he was the killer. In addition, the Zodiac Killer threatened to kill school children on a bus and wrote, *"just shoot out the front tire & then pick off the kiddies as they come bouncing out."*

On June 19th, 1970, Police Sgt. Richard Radetich was shot in the head with a .38 caliber handgun while sitting in his patrol car, writing a parking ticket. In another letter to a newspaper, the killer said, *"I shot a man sitting in a parked car with a .38."* The killer continued writing to the media with letters and greeting cards taunting the police and public.

Donna Lass worked as a Nurse at the Sierra Tahoe Casino. On September 6th , 1970, she finished her shift at 2am and was never seen again. In one of his notorious letters to the media, on March 22nd, 1971, the Zodiac took credit for killing Donna Lass and hiding her body. Things were quiet for about three years, until January 29th, 1974, when the Zodiac once again sent a letter to the Chronicle praising the movie, "The Exorcist," as the best comedy that he had ever seen.

The case of the Zodiac Killer has been investigated by numerous people officially and unofficially for over forty years. The murder cases remain open to this day with the SFPD, Napa County, Solano County, and the California Justice Department.

Chapter 44
The Original Night Stalker
Ventura, Dana Point and Irvine California (50+ Victims)

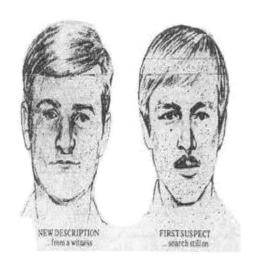

NEW DESCRIPTION
from a witness

FIRST SUSPECT
search still on

It all started in Southern California in December of 1979 and continued to at least May of 1986. I will refer to the Original Night Stalker as ONS.

In a condo in Goleta California on December 30th, 1979, Debra Manning, thirty-five, and Dr. Robert Offerman, forty-four, were found shot to death in bed.

Some neighbors thought they'd heard gunfire, but weren't sure and never reported it. The killer had actually brought along his German Shepherd, and after he had shot the couple he fed the dog leftover turkey. He then went next door, which was vacant, and stole a bike. The neighbor, who happened to be an FBI Agent, heard the noise and gave chase on foot, but the ONS abandoned the bike and ran off.

On March 13th, 1980, another couple was found murdered in their home. Lyman Smith, forty-three, and Charlene Smith, thirty-three, were beaten to death with a fireplace log, and bound with drapery cords on their ankles and wrists. Then, again in 1980, on August 19th, newlyweds, Patrice Harrington, twenty-seven, and her husband Keith, twenty-four, were beaten to death in their home in Dana Point.

The following year there was another home attack and this time only the woman was home because her husband was in hospital recuperating from an illness. On February 6th, 1981, Manuela Witthuhn, twenty-eight, was murdered in her home in Irvine. Her body showed signs of being tied before being beaten, but no ligature marks or murder weapons were found at the scene. It was believed that the ONS tried to make it look like a botched robbery, as he left her TV in the backyard, and stole a crystal curio and lamp.

Just five months later in Goleta on July 26th, 1981, the ONS went to the home of Gregory Sanchez, twenty-seven, and Cheri Domingo, thirty-five, and brought along his German Shepherd again, as shown through trace evidence. Both victims were shot to death and Gregory's body was found in the closet. Neighbors heard no gunshots even though the houses were close together.

There was a five year break between kills, but potentially not. Ten murders were linked through the dog's DNA, but it is suspected the ONS killed approximately fifty people. Janelle Cruz was only eighteen years old, and home alone as her family was in Mexico on vacation. On May 4th, 1986 the ONS entered her home and beat her to death with a pipe wrench.

Some Law Enforcement authorities guesstimate that the ONS's combined total number of victims is around fifty, including his rape victims in Sacramento County and Contra Costa County, and his murder and rape victims in Ventura, Dana Point, and Irvine, California. In the beginning, the ONS was actually called the East Area Rapist and was believed to be responsible for the raping of almost 100 women. He would target females living alone, but escalated his modus operandi and moved on to couples and killing; hence he is called the Original Night Stalker.

It is interesting to note that the East Area Rapist/Original Night Stalker case was the determining factor in the passage of legislation leading to the organization of California's DNA database which authorizes the collection of DNA from all accused and convicted felons in California. California's DNA data retrieval and storage program is considered by experts to be second only to Virginia's in size and effectiveness in solving cold cases. Ironically, while the California DNA database motivated by this case has solved numerous previously unsolved cold cases across the country, the original case remains unsolved.

Chapter 45
The I-45 Killer
Houston, Texas
(34+ Victims)

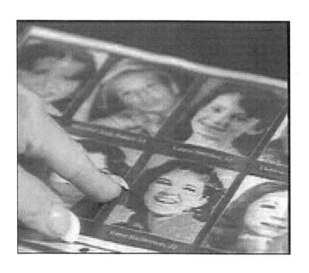

There is a 50-mile stretch between Houston and Galveston, Texas called the Interstate 45. Over three decades, starting in 1971, thirty-two or more women have been killed or dumped on the side of the road. Through evidence from various crime scenes, differences in patterns, and differences in trace data, it is believed by

Special Agent in Charge Don Clark of the Houston office of the FBI, that there may actually be multiple serial killers operating in that area. If that is true, it would be more difficult in catching the UNSUBs.

The authorities believe the interstate to be a dumping site, not the crime scenes where the women were killed. It is an easy place to hide bodies due to the terrain, small country roads, bayous, oak and pine trees, and small towns. The victims usually disappear while out alone. Weeks, sometimes months later, they are found dead in an isolated location somewhere along the interstate. The killer or killers do not leave hints of motive or identification.

The latest victim was discovered in 1999 when a little boy and his dog were out for a walk in some marshy woods. The dog came up with a bone, and then the boy saw a skull. Nearby, the police later found earrings, shreds of clothing, and a belt tied around a tree. Investigators believe the killer used it to bind the young woman while he sexually assaulted her.

Police have a suspect, and have been following him very closely, but they have not publicly identified him.

League City Lt. Gary Ratliff said, *"We know a guy, we know him very well, a guy who has killed before and who had some kind of contact with five of the girls, but all the evidence is circumstantial."*

"The unnamed suspect suffered physical injuries in an automobile accident a few years ago and appears to have gone dormant since then," Ratliff said. While that is good news in one sense, his lack of activity makes it less likely he might commit a mistake that would allow him to be caught.

Chapter 46
Colonial Parkway Killer
Colonial Parkway, Virginia
(8 Victims)
The picture is of the eight victims

These killings happened over twenty-five years ago, though a good update follows the end of the story.

Eight murders happened between 1986 and 1989 along the Colonial Parkway in Virginia. A lesbian couple, Rebecca Dowski, twenty-one, and Cathleen

Thomas, twenty-seven, liked to park on the Colonial Parkway for privacy. On October 12th, 1986, they were found dead inside Thomas's car, which had been pushed down the embankment. There were signs of strangulation and rope burns, and both had had their throats slashed. The motive was not robbery as their money and purses were not taken, nor was there any sexual assault. The only good thing that came of the tragedy came from Cathleen Thomas managing to pull a clump of the suspect's hair, a clump which remained in her hand.

Robin Edwards, fourteen, and David Knobling, twenty, intended to watch a drive-in movie on September 19th, 1987, but when the movie was rained out they went to an arcade. The last time they were seen was on the shore of the James River near Smithfield, Virginia. Later, they were found executed and dumped in the river.

Seven months later, on April 9th, 1988, Cassandra Hailey, eighteen, and Richard Call, on their first date, were reported missing after attending a party in Newport News. Richard's empty car was found on the Colonial Parkway the next day with the door open, keys in still in the ignition, and clothes on the backseat. Neither of their bodies have ever been found, but both are presumed dead.

Anna Phelps, eighteen, and Daniel Lauer, twenty-one, were last seen alive on September 5th, 1989, when they left a rest stop on Interstate 64 in New Kent County. Their skeletal remains were found months later, in October, by hunters a mile from the rest stop. Both were stabbed; the car keys were in the ignition; the gas tank was almost full; Anna's purse was in the car, and police found no sign of struggle.

Authorities seem to think that the killer is in law enforcement or is someone impersonating a police officer.

In January of 2010, some crime scene photos of the Parkway murder victims were inappropriately used to instruct a class by a retired FBI photographer. These pictures leaked to the media and subsequently the investigation was re-opened. Investigators soon discovered dozens of pieces of evidence stored away for over twenty years that had never been tested for DNA. The FBI met with the victim's families after much criticism from the media and had all the evidence sent to the crime lab at Quantico for DNA scrutiny. The families were told that the testing would take some time and continue into 2011.

Update: October 19th, 2011 – Lynn-Marie Carty is a famous national private detective. There is no doubt in her mind that Michael Nicholaou is the Colonial Parkway Killer and she is working diligently to prove it. The FBI is now testing his DNA for comparison.

You can read her story at this site: http://parkway.crimeshadows.com/nicholaou.htm

Chapter 47
The Babysitter Killer
Oakland County, Michigan
(4-5 Victims)

VICTIMS OF THE OAKLAND COUNTY CHILD KILLER 1976-77

Mark Stebbins   Jill Robinson   Kristine Mihelich   Timothy King

In 1976, an unidentified killer stalked Oakland County, Michigan, preying on inhabited children. The killer was nicknamed "The Babysitter" due to the abundant care he provided his young victims while he held them captive before murdering them.

Of the six victims accredited to The Babysitter Killer, two were raped. The corpses of four of the children were washed clean and carefully laid on the fresh snow. The obsessive scrubbing of the corpses suggested that the killer could have been practicing some type of purification rite, or simply removing any incriminating evidence.

Because of the diverse killing methods used by the attacker, authorities initially believed they were searching for up to four different killers; however, by the sixth victim, eleven-year-old Timothy King, police started to believe that they were searching for one killer. After Tim's disappearance, his mother went on television promising the boy his favorite chicken if he returned home. But Tim never made it back home alive. The killer, however, did feed him a chicken dinner before suffocating him.

A Detroit psychiatrist published an open letter in March of 1977 directed to the killer theorizing on the killer's motives for preying on children. Of the many responses he received, one stood out: "The article was wrong you better hope it doesn't snow anymore." The psychiatrist received more letters from a man calling himself Allen who claimed that his roommate was the mysterious killer. Both men were Vietnam vets, and he claimed buddy was targeting suburban children in his war against affluent America.

There were no more deaths attributed to The Babysitter. Authorities believe the killer might have retired, died, moved, or become incarcerated for an unrelated crime. Perhaps he moved to warmer climates where he never again saw fresh snow.

In the 1980s, suspicion focused on a former Warren autoworker in Norberg when, among his belongings, relatives found a cross inscribed with the first name of a victim, Kristine. Although he died in a car wreck in 1981, on August 29th, 1999, Michigan authorities announced they were going to his exhume his grave in Wyoming and take DNA samples to match it against a hair found on the body of one of his suspected victims. This turned out to be negative.

Chapter 48
The Highway of Tears Killer
Highway 16 – Yellowhead
British Columbia
(40+ Victims)

Along a 500-mile section of highway between Prince George and Prince Rupert, British Columbia, Canada, at least forty-three young women have disappeared since 1969. This section of road is now called the Highway of Tears, and a website has been launched in the victims honor by Prince George businessperson Tony Romeyn, who was moved by the stories of women who have gone missing along Highway 16, and wanted to help the families of the victims.

http://www.highwayoftears.ca/website %20Launched.htm

On the site, there is a map of Highway 16 that shows the general area where nineteen victims were found or is said to have disappeared. Four of the nineteen girls are listed as missing, while the bodies of the other fifteen have been found and the cases considered homicides. Ann Bascu, who went missing in 1983, is the only one who went missing outside of B.C., in Hinton, Alta.

The RCMP, or the Royal Canadian Mounted Police, have examined the similarities among the murders and disappearances and have ascertained that eighteen of the victims share positive links.

The Highway of Tears Symposium was held in March 2006 by several Prince

George-area aboriginal groups. The outcome was the Highway of Tears Symposium Recommendation Report, published June 2006. It states:

"There is much community speculation and debate on the exact number of women that have disappeared along Highway 16 over a longer 35 year period; many are saying the number of missing women, combined with the number of confirmed murdered women, exceeds 30." The report says the term Highway of Tears was the result of the "fear, frustration, and sorrow" that grew "within First Nations communities along the highway upon each reported case of a young woman's disappearance, or confirmation of a recovered body."

Chapter 49
Serial Killers
Famous Last Words

"I'd just like to say I'm sailing with the rock, and I'll be back like 'Independence Day,' with Jesus June 6. Like the movie, big mother ship and all, I'll be back."
- Aileen Wuornos

"Kiss my ass".
- John Wayne Gacy

"Let's do it".
- Gary Gilmore

"Hurry it up you Hoosier bastard! I could hang a dozen men while you're screwing around".
- Carl Panzram

"I'd like you to give my love to my family and friends."
- Ted Bundy

Dr. H. H. Holmes and the Whitechapel Ripper

by Dane Ladwig
http://www.holmestheripper.com

In 1888, in the East End of London, the heart of the Whitechapel district was crippled by the crimes of a fiendish murderer known as Jack the Ripper. Across the ocean, in America, another monster was on the loose – Dr. H. H. Holmes.

The mystery of the unsolved Jack the Ripper murders would puzzle the world for the next century and the years ahead. Scotland Yard Detectives, Stockholm's finest minds, criminologist and experts (or "Ripperologists") all endeavored and failed to unravel the mysterious identity of the world's most notorious serial killer.

After more than a century of conjecture and inconclusive theories, the Ripper's identity is no less a mystery than it was at the time of the murders. Is it possible Scotland Yard investigators were correct after all? Could the notorious Ripper have been an American visiting London? Furthermore, is it possible the visiting Ripper was an American physician and convicted serial killer?

In Dr. H. H. Holmes and the Whitechapel Ripper, the unproven propositions regarding the possible identity of Jack the Ripper are considered and weighed against the facts. Theory and literature based on opinion and imagination are left aside as only the facts and reason are considered.

The Historian, student, Ripperologist, or simply those intrigued with perhaps the greatest of all unsolved mysteries, should add to their knowledge with what is revealed in this compelling account of Dr. H. H. Holmes and the Whitechapel Ripper.

CONTENT

Serial Killer Defined 7
Organized or Disorganized 12
Capturing Serial Killers 19
Female Serial Killers 24
The Black Widows 28
The Angels of Death 35
Sexual Predators and Revenge 38
Murder for Profit 41
Female Team Killers 43
Issue of Sanity 50
The Unexplained Killer 53
The Unsolved Killings 58
Gertrude Baniszewki 60
Margie Barfield 64
Martha Beck 69
Lizzie Borden 73
Judias Buenoano 78
Christine Falling 89
Caril Ann Fugate 93
de Jesus Gonzalez sisters 100
Karla Homolka 103
Dorothea Puente 113
Marybeth Tinning 118
Rosemary West 123
John Wayne Gacy 127
Ted Bundy 143
Donald Henry Gaskins 160

Gary Ridgway 166

Jeffrey Dahmer 174

Dennis Rader 184

David Berkowitz 199

The D.C. Snipers 212

Tsutomu Miyazaki 219

Andrei Chikatilo 224

Ottis Toole / Henry Lee Lucas 248

Doctors Who Killed Preface 255

Dr. Joseph Michael Swango 257

Dr. Marcel Petiot 272

Dr. Harold Frederick Shipman 282

Dr. H. H. Holmes 292

Dr. John Bodkin Adams 304

Unsolved Serial Murder Cases Preface 327

The Zodiac Killer 328

Original Night Stalker 335

The I-45 Killer 339

Colonial Parkway Killer 342

The Babysitter Killer 346

The Highway of Tears Killer 349

Serial Killers Famous Last Words 352

Dr. H. H. Holmes and the Whitechapel Ripper 353

)

6270346R00192

Made in the USA
San Bernardino, CA
04 December 2013